How to Do a Dissertation in Record Time Using Government Data

How to Do a Dissertation in Record Time Using Government Data

A Primer

Robert O. Slater

ROWMAN & LITTLEFIELD
Lanham • Boulder • New York • London

Published by Rowman & Littlefield
An imprint of The Rowman & Littlefield Publishing Group, Inc.
4501 Forbes Boulevard, Suite 200, Lanham, Maryland 20706
www.rowman.com

86-90 Paul Street, London EC2A 4NE

Copyright © 2024 by Robert O. Slater

All rights reserved. No part of this book may be reproduced in any form or by any electronic or mechanical means, including information storage and retrieval systems, without written permission from the publisher, except by a reviewer who may quote passages in a review.

British Library Cataloguing in Publication Information Available

Library of Congress Cataloging-in-Publication Data

Names: Slater, Robert (Robert O.) author.
Title: How to do a dissertation in record time using government data: a primer / Robert Slater.
Description: Lanham, Maryland: Rowman & Littlefield Publishers, [2024] | Includes bibliographical references. | Summary: "A practical, commonsense, how-to guide to writing a doctoral dissertation that shows beginner students how to use government data to cut months, even years off of the process"—Provided by publisher.
Identifiers: LCCN 2024030941 (print) | LCCN 2024030942 (ebook) | ISBN 9781610485692 (cloth) | ISBN 9781610485715 (ebook)
Subjects: LCSH: Dissertations, Academic. | Report writing. | Administrative agencies—Data processing.
Classification: LCC LB2369.S58 2024 (print) | LCC LB2369 (ebook) | DDC 808.06/6378—dc23/eng/20240708
LC record available at https://lccn.loc.gov/2024030941
LC ebook record available at https://lccn.loc.gov/2024030942

Contents

Chapter 1: Introduction   1
Chapter 2: Doctoral Program Overview   7
Chapter 3: The Structure of the Traditional Dissertation   13
Chapter 4: Ten Commonsense Questions   17
Chapter 5: The Practical and Theoretical Questions   21
Chapter 6: From "Topic" to Research Question   27
Chapter 7: Problem Statement   33
Chapter 8: Literature Review and Conceptual Framework   43
Chapter 9: Methodology   49
Chapter 10: Data Analysis and Discussion   59
Chapter 11: Summary, Conclusions and Recommendations   65
Chapter 12: The Mind's Eye   69

Appendix A: Accessing the GSS and NAEP Data   71
References   77
About the Author   79

For my families

Chapter 1

Introduction

PURPOSE OF THE BOOK

This book is written to help students in the social sciences and education do their dissertations in as few as four years from start to finish, from their first doctoral course to the final defense of their dissertation. Its purpose is to show doctoral students how to conceptualize, formulate, and investigate a research problem using government data. Two data sets will be used. One is the General Social Survey (GSS). This data set is used by social scientists the world over and contains some of the best information available on American society. The other data used in this book is from the National Assessment of Educational Progress (NAEP), the gold standard for data on US K–12 education. Both sets of data are free and available 24/7 online.[1] These, of course, are not the only government data sets that students might use for their research, but they are among the best available on American society and education.

The General Social Survey is a personal interview survey of Americans age eighteen and older. This survey, or set of surveys, has been done since 1972. "It is the only full-probability, personal-interview survey designed to monitor changes in both social characteristics and attitudes currently being conducted in the United States."[2] In no other set of data can doctoral students find more information on Americans' backgrounds, on how they spend their time, and on what they believe about God, home, work, politics, sex, and a myriad of others issues. The GSS is, quite simply, a doctoral student's gold mine. It can not only shorten their doctoral program by years and enable them to avoid a lengthy Institutional Review Board proposal,[3] but it can also result in a piece of work that is publishable in the most respected journals in the social sciences.

The National Assessment of Educational Progress or NAEP, is to doctoral students in K–12 education what the GSS is to doctoral students in the social sciences. As the NAEP website explains:

> The National Assessment of Educational Progress (NAEP)—a congressionally mandated large-scale assessment administered by the National Center for Education Statistics (NCES)—consists of print and digital assessments in various subject areas. Three of these subjects—mathematics, reading, and science—are assessed most frequently and reported at the state and select district level, usually for grades 4 and 8. The Nation's Report Card provides results on student performance based on gender, race/ethnicity, public or nonpublic school, teacher experience, and hundreds of other factors.[4]

The NAEP enables doctoral students to examine a host of relationships between school factors, teacher variables, teaching methods and curricula, and student achievement, and in all the major subjects. As with the GSS, students who use the NAEP data to do their dissertations will likely finish faster than students who collect their own data. Moreover, their use of NAEP can also result in a publishable piece of work in record time.

To introduce doctoral students to these two data sets, and to show them how they can be used to conceptualize, formulate, and investigate a research problem in the social sciences or education, two general topics will be used as examples. One topic is "educational attainment."

Educational attainment is here understood as the amount of formal education that an individual manages to attain. This is or should be an important topic not only for doctoral students in education but also for many in the social sciences. As the reader will discover, if they are not already familiar with the fact, educational attainment is correlated with many other individual characteristics and behaviors. For example, the amount of formal education that Americans attain is correlated with their race, class, and gender. Also, Americans' educational attainment influences such things as their choice of marriage partner and their participation in politics. So, educational attainment is a good topic to show doctoral students how to use the GSS to conceptualize, formulate, and investigate a doctoral research problem.

The second topic is "student achievement." This topic should be of particular interest to doctoral students in K–12 education. Most of the discussion in contemporary K–12 education comes down to the general question of what schools and educators can do to improve student learning, particularly student achievement in reading, mathematics, and science. Student achievement is also not only a topic of national interest but international import as well. The United States is and should be concerned about how its K–12 students fare in comparison with students from other countries. As international data indicate, we are, at best, behind a dozen or so other countries in some important achievement areas. So, student achievement is a good topic to use to show doctoral students in K–12 education how to use NAEP data to conceptualize, formulate, and investigate a research problem.

LEARNING HOW TO THINK

At this point, the reader may be under the impression that this book is only useful for those interested in doing a "quantitative" dissertation. This, however, is a misunderstanding of what this book is about. It is not simply intended to show students how to use archival data to shorten their time in a doctoral program while simultaneously producing a good, professional piece of work. It is also designed to help students learn how to think as a researcher thinks when they are trying to figure out what they want to know and investigate.

The most important goal of a good doctoral program is not only to give students knowledge but to teach them how to think. It is thinking that produces knowledge. In teaching students how to think, a doctoral program teaches them how to be knowledge producers and not just knowledge consumers; it shows them not only how to participate in a knowledge society but also gives them the means to advance it. Thinking, especially thinking like a researcher, should be the most important skill they acquire. But what does "thinking" mean in this context?

This book takes a pragmatic approach to thinking, an approach informed by the philosophers Charles Pierce, William James, John Dewey, and George Herbert Mead. Put in a nutshell, these philosophers believed that thinking is in fact doing. It is not passive. It is not, for example, what is depicted by Rodin's famous work The Thinker.[5] When people think, these philosophers suggested, they are not passively sitting in deep thought, contemplating themselves, the world, and the universe. They are acting, trying to solve a problem, trying this solution and then another, trying to figure out what works. By using the GSS or NAEP data, students have an opportunity to test a variety of hypotheses about what affects educational attainment and student achievement and what their consequences are for other variables.

Pragmatically speaking, then, thinking at the doctoral level comes down to systematically formulating and trying to answer questions, and not just any questions but questions that get at the essence of what they are trying to understand and know. Important questions in the case of educational attainment and student achievement are: What correlates with their variation? Which correlates are logically prior to these two variables, and which are logically consequences?

A good doctoral program entails a complex process involving many things but this book focuses only on one thing, albeit the most important: the doctoral dissertation. Unfortunately, in too many doctoral programs thinking about the dissertation comes last, after course work and comprehensive exams. In the best programs, however, thinking about the dissertation comes first and last. The dissertation is made both the start and the culmination of everything. It becomes the proof that the student has transformed herself from mere knowledge consumer to knowledge producer. In sum, the best doctoral programs begin with the end—the dissertation—and strive to make everything else a means to that end.

So, the reader of this book will not find here what they will find in most other books that treat of doctoral programs and the process of getting a doctorate. Not much if anything is said about how to decide what to study, which doctoral programs to apply for or how to gain admission to them. Nor is there much about how to deal with the problem of navigating the twenty or so courses that comprise most programs or preparing for the comprehensive exams or "comps." The focus here is on the doctoral dissertation, particularly on how to think about and conceptualize the dissertation, and to use real data to do it.

ORGANIZATION OF CHAPTERS

The structure of the book follows from its objective. The second chapter is a brief overview of the main elements of most doctoral programs, elements that other books often take multiple chapters to cover. The goal here is to convey a general sense of the process as opposed to detail.

Chapter 2 gives a brief overview of the basic requirements found in most doctoral programs.

Chapter 3 introduces the standard five-part dissertation structure. Here, each of the five chapters that comprise many if not most dissertations are briefly outlined. These are 1) Problem Statement, 2) Literature Review and Conceptual Framework, 3) Methodology, 4) Data Analysis and Discussion, and 5) Summary, Conclusions, and Recommendations.

Chapter 4 focuses on the commonsense questions that inform or lie behind each of the five chapters mentioned above. It is useful to see each of the dissertation's parts or chapters as an attempt to answer a set of commonsense questions. These questions can serve as constant guides to the researcher. They can be used as reminders of what it is that he or she wants to know and why it is worth knowing, of what others before them have found out about their topic, of what they did to find out, and what was left to be done.

Chapter 5 introduces a distinction between theoretical and practical questions. This distinction is meant to remind the student that while their research may be motivated by a practical concern, a dissertation question is usually theoretical not practical in nature. This is not to say that practical concerns cannot be addressed. They can, but normally not as the main research question in the study. The exception to this is when the study is intended to be an evaluation of some project.

Chapter 6 shows how to use the theoretical questions to formulate a problem statement and relational hypotheses.

Chapter 7 deals with the problem statement, the most important part of the dissertation, and usually is its opening chapter. Here the focus is on how to think about one's research topic—any topic, really—and turn it into an acceptable research problem. The student is shown how to do this by systematically subjecting a topic to the theoretical and practical questions.

Chapter 8 of the book focuses on the literature review and conceptual framework. The literature review is driven by the primary and secondary questions developed in the problem statement. It is a prelude to the conceptual framework of the study. This, in simple terms, is a statement of how the main phenomena in the study, the main constructs and concepts, are interrelated.

Chapter 9 takes up methodological concerns. It briefly summarizes the basic methodological choices, research design, data description, IRB issues and related matters.

Chapter 10 suggests an approach to the presentation of data and tables that is consistent with the principle of parsimony.

Chapter 11 touches upon some issues related to the summary of the research, articulation of the main conclusions, and recommendations for further research.

Chapter 12 reviews the role that the commonsense questions and the theoretical and practical questions play in the development of a research project.

NOTES

1. See https://gss.norc.org/ for information about the General Social Survey, and see https://nces.ed.gov/nationsreportcard/ for information about the National Assessment of Educational Progress.

2. https://gss.norc.org/About-The-GSS

3. An Institutional Review Board (IRB) is a university committee that reviews proposals for research that involves the use and protection of human subjects.

4. The Nation's Report Card, U.S. Department of Education, 2024. https://www.nationsreportcard.gov/faq.aspx

5. I am indebted, for the Rodin example, to D. C. Phillips, who uses it in his *A Companion to John Dewey's Democracy and Education* (Chicago: University of Chicago Press, 2016), a superb discussion of Dewey's classic book.

Chapter 2

Doctoral Program Overview

As its title suggests, the focus of this book is on the doctoral dissertation, particularly on how to think about a dissertation, and especially on how to ask and address the questions that thinking involves.

Undergraduate and master's programs are mainly designed to give students knowledge. The best doctoral programs, however, are designed to teach students how to create knowledge. Knowledge is a product of thinking. Learning how to think, therefore, particularly learning how to think like a researcher and to ask the right questions, is the key to success in a doctoral program.

As teaching students how to think about and do their dissertations is the main focus of this book, only the most general advice is given here about the structure and content of doctoral programs. What follows are some very general points.

THE BASIC REQUIREMENTS OF A DOCTORAL PROGRAM

Doctoral students, especially in the social sciences, typically have five major milestones in their programs, milestones that students often think of as "challenges" to be met or "hurdles" to be jumped. These are: 1) course work, 2) comprehensive exams or "comps," 3) admission to candidacy, 4) dissertation proposal defense or "hearing," and 5) final dissertation defense. A word about each of these may be helpful.

Coursework

Typically, doctoral students have to take about twenty courses, though some programs may require more. The courses are usually of three types: research courses, subject-specialty courses, and electives. The research courses typically include an introductory course that provides an overview of the research process. Common topics in this course are the basic kinds of research: qualitative, quantitative, and mixed, the last being a combination of the first two. Another topic usually covered has to do with research design. In this case, the student has to decide whether their research will be qualitative, quantitative, or a mix of the two. Quantitative studies can be experimental or nonexperimental.

Subject-specialty courses are those with content related to the subject of the program. So, for example, subject-specialty courses in sociology might focus on stratification, organizations, the sociology of gender or race, and the like. Subject-specialty courses in psychology might focus on personality theory, human development, cognitive processes, abnormal psychology, and so on. The courses in an educational leadership doctoral program will likely include leadership theory, the management of educational organizations, educational policy, and similar. Of the twenty or so courses required in a doctoral program, as many as half will likely be subject-specialty courses. Electives are courses that are not required but students would like to take. They may or may not be in the students' program/department and may even be offered in another college.

Comprehensive Exams

Comprehensive exams or "comps" are given near or at the end of course work. They usually entail one or two questions from each of the student's professors, and these questions generally relate to subject-specialty knowledge. The general purpose of these exams is to assess the student's knowledge of the program's primary subject, that is, they are concerned with how much students actually know about the basics of sociology, psychology, economics, educational leadership, or whatever the program's specialty happens to be.

While most doctoral programs have comprehensive exams, some programs, such as Harvard's educational leadership doctoral program, substitute a substantial paper for the comp exams. Sometimes called a "qualifying" paper, this work can be focused on the student's dissertation topic and may serve as an initial foray into the literature related to the topic. It may or may not be necessary to "defend" this paper.

If it is necessary to defend the qualifying paper, a defense typically consists of two or more professors and the student sitting at a conference table for an hour or more while the professors ask the student questions about the paper's subject and its treatment. At the conclusion of the defense, the professors inform the student as to whether or not they have passed. A "no-pass" vote is not typical. More often, in the case of a "weak" defense, revisions to the paper are required and perhaps even another sit-down session. However, depending on the program's policy, a no-pass could be used to drop the student from the program if the faculty think it warranted.

Admission to Candidacy

Once the student has passed the comprehensive exams or qualifying paper, they are allowed to file the paperwork for candidacy. Becoming a doctoral "candidate" is an important step. It signals to others that the student has completed the preparation for the most important thing in a doctoral program: the dissertation. Upon achieving candidacy status the student is ready to find a dissertation chair and put together a committee.

By the time students have reached the candidacy stage of the doctoral process, they probably have an idea of what faculty members they can work with, and which particular member they would like to have direct their dissertation research. Finding a faculty member to "chair" or lead one's dissertation committee is not simply a matter of asking them whether or not they would be willing to serve as chair. In the best universities, the protocol is to ask by presenting the faculty member with a draft of a problem statement that he or she can read. If the faculty member has no expertise in the student's area of interest they may decline.

More will be said in the following chapters about what a dissertation "problem" consists of but, put simply, it is a general question pertaining to some phenomenon that the student is interested in studying. The research problem should be stated in the form of a question or interrogative statement. This point can hardly be overemphasized. Too many doctoral students fail to formulate their dissertation research in terms of a single overarching or primary question that captures the main lines of their interest. This mistake that can cost students valuable time and even, in the worst case, keep them from completing their dissertation altogether. With some exceptions, pertaining mainly to qualitative research, the clearer the student is at the outset about the question they are trying to answer with their dissertation research, the easier their work will be.

Once a faculty member agrees to chair the dissertation, the student needs to discuss with him or her what other members should be asked to join the committee. Here, the student should pay heed to the chair's wishes, since department politics may make some combinations of faculty difficult. A good dissertation committee chair will not recommend putting anyone on the committee with whom they cannot work or who might create needless difficulties for the student.

The Dissertation Proposal

Once a dissertation chair and committee have been formed and the proper paperwork filed with the graduate school, the student is ready to write the dissertation proposal. This essentially consists of the first three chapters of the dissertation: 1) problem statement, 2) literature review and conceptual framework and 3) methodology. What is contained in the proposal and how long it should be depends on the particular program in which the student is working. Some programs require only a short literature review while in others the entire review is preferred.

When the chair and the rest of the committee members believe the proposal is ready, the chair sets a date for a proposal "hearing" or, more formally, a defense. Again, the procedure usually involves a sit-down with the committee members and the student for a discussion of the proposal. This discussion may be formal or informal, depending on local policy. The more formal it is, the more it becomes a defense, and the less formal, the more it takes the form of a hearing. The difference between the two essentially comes down to purpose: Does the faculty wish to grill the student? Alternatively, do they simply want to make sure that the research design and proposal is sound and capable of being done in a reasonable amount of time, and that successful completion of the study is a likely outcome? The more the first intent is emphasized, the more the process becomes a defense, while an emphasis on the second makes for a hearing.

Upon getting the committee's approval to proceed with the research and the writing of the final dissertation report, the student submits a proposal to the institution's Institutional Review Board. This is an administrative body charged with the protection of the rights and welfare of human research subjects recruited to participate in research activities conducted under the auspices of the institution with which the student is affiliated. IRB approval is necessary for the protection of human subjects, should any be involved in the research. In general, if the student chooses to use archival data, IRB approval is normally swift. If, on the other hand, human subjects are to be interviewed or studied, especially children, the approval process is likely to be more complex.

Final Dissertation Defense

The final step or "hurdle" in the doctoral process is the defense of the dissertation itself. Again, this involves a back-and-forth between the student and committee members that can take two to three hours or more. The dissertation defense is almost always formal and usually involves the faculty grilling the student on the design and conduct of their research, their findings, and their recommendations for future research.

Upon successful defense of the final dissertation, the student has, for all practical purposes, achieved the doctorate. Often, upon congratulating the student on a successful defense, the student's committee members will refer to him or her as "Dr."

After a successful defense and any required revisions or made to the dissertation, it must be submitted to the graduate school to be reviewed and formatted according to the criteria of the particular program and university from which the degree is being awarded. Lastly, there are the preparations for graduations: invitations sent, coordination of family, and so on.

The whole doctoral process, depending on the field of study and the higher education institution involved, can take anywhere from four to six or more years to complete.

While the dissertation itself is only one component of the doctoral process, the student will do well to keep in mind that it is the most important. It is the end or purpose toward which everything else in the program should aim. All of the other components in a doctoral program are, in a very real sense, secondary to the final product, which is a more or less lengthy and formally written manuscript on some particular topic of interest to the student.

Chapter 3

The Structure of the Traditional Dissertation

THE FIVE-CHAPTER STRUCTURE

The traditional dissertation has five major parts or chapters. These are:

1. Problem Statement
2. Literature Review and Conceptual Framework
3. Methodology
4. Data Analysis and Discussion
5. Summary, Conclusions and Recommendations

The remaining discussion through this book will assume this traditional five-chapter structure. However, while this is the general structure of most dissertations, it does allow exceptions. In some programs, for example, a separate chapter might be devoted to the conceptual framework. An additional chapter devoted to data analysis could be included as well. But these and other deviations from the traditional structure are usually exceptions to the rule. Most dissertations follow the five-chapter format.

A brief description of each of these chapters may help students to orient themselves to what comes later.

THE PROBLEM STATEMENT CHAPTER

In a problem statement the "problem" should be, in its simplest form, a question about what it is that the researcher wants to know. This is most usefully thought of as a general or "primary" question that captures the phenomenon of interest. The "phenomenon of interest" is the particular "thing" or a "topic" that the student happens to be interested in. We have, for example, chosen two topics or phenomena for this book: educational attainment and student achievement.

If we were to state the research question for each of the two topics, the general or overarching research question for educational attainment might be: What factors influence educational attainment? Or why do some people attain higher degrees while others fail to earn a high school diploma? In the case of student achievement the question might be: What influences student achievement in reading or why do some students have high test scores in reading while others have low scores?

These formulations of the general research question should be considered tentative, a starting formulation. As we reflect on and learn more about educational attainment and student achievement, these ways of putting the general research question are apt to change.

Suppose, for example, that after reading about educational attainment the student wants to know how the educational attainment of parents correlates with the educational attainment of their children. In this instance, the general research question—What factors influence educational attainment?—would be amended to a more specific formulation, perhaps something like this: What is the relationship between parents' education and the educational attainment of their children?

To take the second example, suppose that the student interested in student achievement decides that she is interested in knowing whether children who have a library card tend to score better on reading tests. In this case the initial question—What influences student achievement in reading?—would likely be amended to read: Is there a relationship between having and using a public library card and children's reading scores?

Justifying the Problem

The problem-statement chapter also usually includes a justification for the question. The justification consists of one or more reasons why the primary question is worth asking and investigating. The reasons can be both practical and theoretical in nature.

In this chapter, too, one usually finds a discussion of the research's limitations and delimitations. In simple terms, limitations of the research are things that would be good to have in the study but are not possible to obtain or do. However, the limitations are not serious enough to make the dissertation indefensible. Delimitations are things that could be done but, for one reason or another, the researcher chooses not to do them, usually because they are not absolutely necessary to answer the primary question or to defend the study.

The problem statement chapter may also include a list of key terms and their definitions, though some researchers will provide the definitions of key terms as they introduce them in the narrative itself.

Finally, sometimes the problem statement will also include hypotheses, especially if the study is more quantitative in nature. As will be explained in due course, hypotheses can be either direct or propositional in nature or of the null variety. More will be said on this in what follows.

THE LITERATURE REVIEW AND CONCEPTUAL FRAMEWORK CHAPTER

The literature review is an organized and systematic critical discussion of the most important and relevant research that has been done on the topic or primary research question. It is an effort to summarize in an accessible way what is already known about the topic being investigated or the specific question that the researcher has posed about the topic.

The conceptual framework is essentially a logical model or schema of how the main phenomenon of interest is related to other things that influence it or that it influences. In a quantitative study this logical model is used to guide statistical analyses and the discussion of how the various things in the model are correlated and intercorrelated.

THE METHODOLOGY CHAPTER

The methodology chapter of the dissertation describes and justifies the research design chosen to investigate the question at hand. It informs the reader as to whether the study is quantitative, qualitative, or of a mixed-methods approach. It also gives information about the data used to address the primary research question, detailing how the data were collected and the instrument(s) used to collect them. This chapter also discusses the IRB or the application made to the University's Institutional Review Board to gain permission to study human subjects. It usually also presents the main methods used to analyze the data and, in a quantitative study, lists the variables in the study, their definitions and measures.

THE DATA ANALYSIS AND DISCUSSION CHAPTER

This chapter walks the reader through the analysis of the data using the primary research question and its associated secondary questions to guide the analysis. If the research design is for a quantitative study, one or more tables and figures are typically used to present the findings. If a qualitative study is being done, this chapter will likely involve quotes from individuals interviewed or observed.

THE SUMMARY, CONCLUSIONS, AND RECOMMENDATIONS CHAPTER

The fifth and typically final chapter of the dissertation restates the primary question behind the study. It then follows with the main findings about the question that flow from the data analysis. Next come the conclusions that can be drawn from these findings and their qualifications. These are followed by any recommendations for future research that the student deems warranted.

Chapter 4

Ten Commonsense Questions

Each of the five parts or chapters of the traditional dissertation has associated with it one or more commonsense questions. A dissertation is a complex piece of work. It often involves a number of technical details. It often entails reviews of more than one body of literature. It is easy to get lost in the morass of information one accumulates when trying to write it. Accordingly, it is helpful to have some commonsense reminders of what each part is supposed to do, irrespective of the subject or topic involved. These aids are here presented as a series of questions that students can use throughout the writing process to maintain their orientation. These questions are here referred to as the "common sense" questions. What follows is a brief introduction to them and suggestions as to how they might help students to keep in mind what they are about as they work on each chapter.

THE PROBLEM STATEMENT

What do I want to know, and why is it worth knowing?

    The commonsense question that guides the problem statement emphasizes two points. The first is that a dissertation is a research activity, and the point of research is to get knowledge. The second point is that the knowledge sought should be worth seeking. This is to say that students needs to have one or more reasons for doing the work required to obtain the knowledge sought. When it comes to their dissertations, then, doctoral students need to figure out, at least generally, what they want to know and why it is worth knowing in the first place.

Example: Educational Attainment and Student Achievement

The commonsense question in the case of educational attainment would be: What do I want to know about educational attainment, and why is it worth knowing? For those students working with student achievement, the commonsense question would be: What do I want to know about student achievement and why is it worth knowing?

LITERATURE REVIEW AND CONCEPTUAL FRAMEWORK

Who else besides me has wanted to know what I want to know or something like I want to know? What did they find out and what did they do to find out? Given what they found out, what is my best guess as to what I am going to find when I do my investigation?

The first two of these commonsense questions guide the literature review. The third pertains to the conceptual framework. The first two questions are meant to direct the students' energies to finding studies that are similar to the ones they are thinking about doing, studies wherein the principal investigator has asked a similar or even the same question that they have formulated.

Most topics that doctoral students want to investigate have been investigated before. It is very likely that whatever primary question is asked, it has been asked previously. Commonsense question 4 guides the conceptual framework. Put simply, a conceptual framework consists of one or more verbal statements or visuals describing how the phenomenon of interest—the "thing" that students are interested in—is related to other phenomena that are believed to correlate with it.

Example: Educational Attainment and Student Achievement

For educational attainment the commonsense questions here would be: Who else besides me has wanted to know what I want to know about educational attainment, what did they find out and what did they do to find out? Given what they found out about educational attainment, what is my best guess about what I am going to find? Similarly, the commonsense question for student achievement would be: Who else besides me has wanted to know what I want to know about student achievement, what did they find out, and what did they do to find out? Given what they found out about student achievement, what is my best guess about what I am going to find?

METHODOLOGY

Given what I want to know about, and what others before me have found out about it, what am I actually going to do to find out what I want to know?

As already noted, the most important work of a dissertation is the work of thinking, the work of figuring out what the question is that must be answered. To answer the question posed, thinking is not enough. Action needs to be taken. Data of some sort must be collected and analyzed. What kind of data must be collected, how it is to be collected, and how it will analyzed are all questions dealt with in the methodology chapter. Here, students must have in mind a clear plan of action. Will interviews be done? Survey constructed, piloted, and administered? Observations made? These and related questions are methodological in nature.

Example: Educational Attainment and Student Achievement

For educational attainment, the question here is: Given what others before me have found out about educational attainment, what am I going to actually do to find out what I want to know about it? For student achievement it is: Given what others before me have found out about student achievement, what am I going to actually do to find out what I want to know about it?

DATA ANALYSIS AND DISCUSSION

What did I find out about what I want to know and what evidence do I have?

In this chapter the student once again poses the primary and secondary questions addressing each with data, qualitative or quantitative.

Example: Educational Attainment and Student Achievement

The questions here are: What did I find out about educational attainment and what evidence do I have? What did I find out about student achievement and what evidence do I have?

Chapter 4

SUMMARY, CONCLUSIONS, AND RECOMMENDATIONS

What did I start out wanting to know?
What did I find out?
So, what?
What more has to be done?

Example: Educational Attainment and Student Achievement

The commonsense questions here are: What did I start out wanting to know about educational attainment? What did I find out about it? So what? What more needs to be done? Also, What did I start out wanting to know about student achievement? What did I find out about it? So what? What more needs to be done?

Now, these commonsense questions are not meant to be explicitly stated in the dissertation itself but are rather intended as informal guides to the work. A dissertation is a formal report and these questions are too informal to be included. Nonetheless, students would do well to always keep them in mind as they work through the various chapters. These questions can serve to remind students what they need to do in each chapter and can help prevent drifting too far from the task at hand.

Chapter 5

The Practical and Theoretical Questions

As previously noted, the aim of educational research is to generate knowledge. In this, educational research is no different from research in other fields. The purpose of research in astronomy, for example, is to generate knowledge about celestial objects—planets, stars—and their relationships. In physics, it is to know about the nature and properties of matter and energy. In the social sciences it is to know about human beings and their relationships, groups, and societies. The purpose of educational research is to know about teaching and learning—what they are, how and why they are carried out, how and why they are organized in particular ways, and the consequences of organizing them in one way as opposed to another.

As all research, including educational research, is about generating knowledge, it may be useful to say at the outset how the term "knowledge" is used here and how it should be understood. Epistemologists, those who study knowledge, often make a distinction between two types of knowledge. One type is "practical" knowledge, and the other "theoretical" knowledge. Each type of knowledge is gained by addressing and answering a particular set of questions.

THE PRACTICAL (KNOWLEDGE) QUESTIONS

Practical knowledge is gained by addressing and answering the following kinds of practical questions:

- PQ1. What is to be done?
- PQ2. Who is to do it?
- PQ3. What is the most effective way to do it, that is, the way most likely to achieve the objective or get the job done?

PQ4. What is the most efficient way to do it, that is, the way that will get the job done with the least amount of time or resources?

PQ5. Having decided on the what, who, when, and how of getting the job done, and having acted on these decisions, how well is it working, that is, how well is the job getting done?

These are the questions that any practical effort must deal with and attempt to answer. For experienced practitioners these questions are likely to be implicit; they do not need to bring them consciously to mind when trying to accomplish something. Nonetheless, whether conscious or not, these questions stand behind any and every practical effort.

The practical questions are devices to help articulate what "ought" to exist, to change reality.

Here are examples of the thought process prompted by the practical questions as they are applied to the topics of educational attainment and student achievement:

PQ1. What is to be done? Educational attainment is to be increased! Student achievement is to be improved!

PQ2. Who is to do it? For educational attainment, individuals have to do it themselves with material and/or nonmaterial support from significant others and economic organizations and governmental agencies; governments and/or nongovernmental organizations (NGOs) have to make educational institutions more accessible and affordable and hold them accountable. In the case of student achievement, students have to commit to lerning and achievement, schools have to provide them the resources—material and nonmaterial—they need to make and sustain their commitment.

PQ3. What is the most effective way to do it, that is, the way most likely to achieve the objective or get the job done? The most effective way for individuals to attain education is to stay in school or with a formal program of study until they complete the program. This effort depends on valuing educational attainment and having the material and nonmaterial and internal and external resources necessary to actualize the value. Ditto for individual student achievement.

PQ4. What is the most efficient way to do it, that is, the way that will get the job done with the least amount of time or resources? *See previous.*

PQ5. Having decided on the what, who, when, and how of getting the job done, and having acted on these decisions, how well is it working, that is, how well is the job getting done? *Periodic informal and formal self-assessments and assessments by others.*

THE THEORETICAL (KNOWLEDGE) QUESTIONS

Theoretical knowledge, on the other hand, involves a different set of questions. The questions in this case are as follows:

TQ1. Does a thing exist?
TQ2. How do I know it exists?
TQ3. What kind of a thing is it?
TQ4. What are its essential characteristics?
TQ5. To what things is it similar and how does it differ from them?
TQ6. How does it vary from one case to the next?
TQ7. What causes it to exist or why does it exist?
TQ8. What are the consequences of its existence?

Now, let us try to imagine the thought process we might go through in applying the theoretical questions (TQ1–TQ8) to educational attainment and student achievement, that is, in taking educational attainment or student achievement as the "thing" or "phenomenon" in which we are interested. What follows is an example of the thought process one might go through in applying each of the theoretical questions to the phenomena or constructs of "educational attainment" and "student achievement."

Example: Educational Attainment

TQ1. Does a thing exist? Yes, educational attainment exists.
TQ2. How do I know it exists? I have experienced educational attainment firsthand in my own case and I have also experienced it secondhand through conversations I have had with others and from the things I have read.
TQ3. What kind of a thing is it? At one level, educational attainment is the amount of education one has acquired informally as well as through schools and schooling, and at a more operational level it is the number of years of school completed and for which credit was granted.
TQ4. What are its essential characteristics? Essential characteristics of educational attainment include the possession of a diploma or certificate indicating the amount of formal schooling attained. It also is manifest in one's knowledge and use of language, that is, the educated tend to speak differently from the uneducated.
TQ5. To what things is it similar and how does it differ from them? Educational attainment is similar to being self-taught, but the latter is absent the formal experience and credentials.

TQ6. How does it vary from one case to the next? In the case of educational attainment, some people have little or none, others have some, and still others have a lot, and everything in between these markers.

TQ7. What causes it to exist, why does it exist or why does it vary? A number of factors appear to influence how much education a person attains including race, class, and gender.

TQ8. What are the consequences of its existence? Educational attainment appears to have a number of economic, political, cultural, and psychological consequences.

Example: Student Achievement

TQ1. Does a thing exist? Yes, student achievement exists.

TQ2. How do I know it exists? I have experienced student achievement firsthand through my own achievement as a student in K–12 classrooms, and I have also experienced it secondhand through conversations with others and from reading about it.

TQ3. What kind of a thing is it? At a conceptual level, student achievement is what has been learned in school, and at a more operational level it is the score one achieves on a test designed to measure what students know of reading, mathematics, science, and other subjects.

TQ4. What are its essential characteristics? Essential characteristics of student achievement include the capability of demonstrating the characteristics found in Benjamin Bloom's Taxonomy that relate to the subject matter in question.[1]

TQ5. To what things is it similar and how does it differ from them? Student achievement, at an operational level, is similar to self-testing to check on what one has learned. Self-checking, however, is more informal.

TQ6. How does it vary from one case to the next? In the case of student achievement, some students have low achievement, others have moderate, and still others have high achievement, and everything in between these markers.

TQ7. What causes it to exist, why does it exist, or why does it vary? A number of factors appear to influence student achievement, including race, class, gender, effort, and teacher quality.

TQ8. What are the consequences of its existence? Student achievement appears to have a number of consequences personal and social consequences.

The point of bringing these theoretical questions to bear on educational attainment and student achievement is to hive examples of how students might take their own topics of interest, the particular "things" they happen to be interested in, and conceptualize them with the help of the theoretical questions. The questions can serve as an organizing device, a way of sorting out the various questions that one can logically ask of a thing in the effort to understand its nature. Doctoral students should try subjecting their topics to the same process and see what they come up with.

Experienced researchers may or may not have these theoretical questions in mind as they go about their research. Nonetheless, as in the practical case, while researchers may or may not be conscious of these theoretical questions as they work, the questions stand behind their research endeavors.

Doctoral students would do well to keep this distinction between practical and theoretical questions in mind as they work on their dissertations. They should use the practical questions to orient their thinking, and the theoretical to help conceptualize their research problem. One of the most challenging research tasks is to figure out exactly what it is that one wants to know and why it is worth knowing in the first place. The practical and theoretical questions can help students to manage this challenge.

Doctoral students often come to their doctoral studies with one or more research topics in mind. Often, their topics are related to their work. Most doctoral students have already begun some type of career and are passed their early twenties, the age at which undergraduates normally achieve their baccalaureate degree. Frequently, the topics that students bring to their doctoral studies are motivated by a practical problem. They have experienced some aspect of the world, usually related to their work, that they find unacceptable, and they want to change it for the better. They want to take what is the case, or at least what is perceived to be the case, and change it to what they and others believe ought to be the case. They want what should be instead of what is. The intolerable "is" and a vision of what "should be" motivates their research interests.

There is nothing wrong with beginning one's doctoral studies with a practical problem/topic in mind, with the practical questions. Ultimately, and if the Pragmatists philosophers are to be believed, all human thought, knowledge, is related to solving practical problems, to some effort to address and answer the practical questions. For example, astronomy, the science of charting the sky, not only served in religious functions and rituals but also began with the practical problem of when to plant crops so that they would be most likely to produce the food needed for survival. Astronomy also addressed the practical need to navigate the oceans safely. Practical concerns and problems have from the beginning motivated inquiry.

However, students will soon discover that they need theoretical knowledge to solve practical problems. Doctoral students in K–12 education, for example, often come to the doctoral program with an interest in raising student achievement scores, usually in the subjects of reading, mathematics, or science. They typically believe that some particular intervention will do the job and are interested in showing that if such-and-such is done, scores will go up. The theoretical questions can help inform their practical goals by giving them a better understanding of the phenomena in which they are interested.

NOTE

1. See Lorin W. Anderson, et al. (Eds.). "A Taxonomy for Learning, Teaching, and Assessing: A Revision of Bloom's Taxonomy of Educational Objectives," 2001.

Chapter 6

From "Topic" to Research Question

The purpose of this chapter is to show doctoral students how to take a topic they happened to be interested in and turn it into a research question or problem. The two topics used in this example will be educational attainment and student achievement.

EXAMPLE: EDUCATIONAL ATTAINMENT

As noted in the previous chapter, most students come to their doctoral programs with specific topics they would like to pursue, and these are often practical in nature because they are connected to their jobs. For example, a student in higher education might have a job at a college or university. Most higher education institutions have a perennial interest in graduation rates and keeping students enrolled in their programs until they graduate. Accordingly, students working in higher education have a natural interest in "educational attainment," though they may not think of it in exactly these terms. Their practical interest, then, is to see students graduate, that is, to promote educational attainment.

The is nothing wrong with starting one's research with a topic grounded in practical experience. The task is to turn the topic into a researchable question. How is this done? It is done by looking at the topic through the "lens" of the theoretical questions covered in the previous chapter.

Higher education doctoral students' might be more likely to achieve their practical goal of increasing educational attainment if they think about their topic—educational attainment—with the theoretical questions discussed in chapter 6, especially questions TQ6 and TQ7. Recall from the previous chapter that TQ6 is: Why does the thing I am interested in vary? TQ7 is: What causes the thing to exist? Or: Why does it exist? These two questions are different ways of asking much the same thing.

Applying TQ6 and TQ7 to the topic of educational attainment raises the following questions: What influences educational attainment? Why does educational attainment vary or, more specifically, why do some students persist in attaining their degree and others do not?

No doubt there are many factors that might influence the amount of formal education or schooling a person manages to attain. These factors could be personal or psychological, such as an individual's confidence in their ability to succeed. They might be financial and relate to a person's ability to pay. They could have to do with family background as students whose parents have college degrees tend to have, in addition to more financial resources, more knowledge of the higher education process itself and can also serve to motivate by example. There are, too, factors related to the school. Some schools have programs that are more supportive of student success than others, especially for first-generation college students. Many things, then, might contribute to a person's educational attainment.

For present purposes, however, let us suppose that the doctoral student decides to address the question of why educational attainment varies by looking at the relationship between parents' education and the educational attainment of their children. In this case, the general questions (TQ6 and TQ7) of why educational attainment varies or what influences it take a more specific formulation, namely: Is there a relationship between parents' educational attainment and the educational attainment of their children?

With this reformulation of TQ6 and TQ7, we no longer have a single thing that we are looking at—educational attainment (of an individual). The reformulation introduces a second "thing" or variable. In this case it is the educational attainment of a person's parents. Thus in reformulating TQ6 and TQ7, that is, in providing "answers" to these two theoretical questions, we turn our interest from not just one thing but two things in relation: an individual's education and the education of their parents. In short, we now have a *relationship* or a connection between two things to explore.

The study of relationships between variables is the essence of research in general and quantitative research in particular. Further, when investigating a relationship, the general aim is to answer two questions about it. First, is there in fact a relationship and, if there is, how strong is it? Second, what is the relationship's direction? As one variable goes up, does the other go up with it or down? When both variables move in the same direction, the relationship is said to be "positive." When they go in opposite directions, that is, when one goes up the other goes down or vice-versa, the relationship is said to be an "inverse" one.

Given our general experience, we would expect the relationship between parents' education and their children's education to be positive. Both variables should move in the same direction. We expect that the higher the parents' education, the higher the children's education. As the first goes up, so also should the second. This, at least, is the hypothesis that common sense suggests. S*trength* and *direction*, then, are the two things we want to know about this and any other relationship we are investigating.

Our expectations about the strength and direction of the relationship between parents' education and that of their children constitute an "hypothesis" about the relationship. Our working, commonsense guess or, in more technical terms, our "hypothesis" is that when we look at the data we will find a positive and fairly strong relationship between the parent-child-educational-attainment relationship. We will examine this relationship in chapter 10 on data analysis and discussion.

EXAMPLE: STUDENT ACHIEVEMENT

A second example of going from interest in a single thing or topic to consideration of the thing's relationship with a second thing can be had by way of consideration of student achievement. Again, reflection on TQ6 and TQ7 leads to consideration of other things to which the "topic" might be connected: What influences student achievement? Why does student achievement vary from one student to the next?

As of this writing, students' confidence in their ability to achieve academically is one factor believed to be related to their academic achievement. So, if students' confidence is supposed to influence their academic achievement, the following question presents itself: Is there a relationship between students' confidence in their ability to achieve academically and their academic achievement? Again, as in the previous example, the task is to find out if there is a relationship and, if there is, the relationship's *strength* and *direction*.

As was the case with educational attainment, with this reformulation of the research question, the research is no longer just about one thing (student achievement) but two things in relationship (students' confidence in their ability to achieve academically or self-efficacy AND their actual academic achievement).

In sum, finding a dissertation problem often comes down to articulating the theoretical questions related to the event, problem or thing—the "topic"—in which students have an interest.

So, students can and should use the commonsense questions to organize their thoughts, to keep themselves on track, to find their way back when lost in the forest of details and technicalities that their dissertation is likely to drop them. No matter how many hundreds of pages it may end up being, no matter how complex the technical question or questions it addresses, students will also be trying to answer these rather straightforward, commonsense questions.

They should also use the theoretical questions to turn their topics into questions that they can use to better understand the nature of the the things they are interested in, and their relation with other things.

One of the first pitfalls that many doctoral students encounter, without really being conscious of it until it is too late, is that of not knowing quite what it is that they want to know. Students have to be clear about what it is they want to know before they can write their dissertation. If they begin writing their dissertations in earnest without being clear about what it is they want to know they will end up going in circles, writing and discarding many pages, and driving themselves and everybody else around them crazy. But how does one figure out what it is one wants to know?

Generally speaking, students start with a topic, some "thing" that they are interested in. If they are doing a dissertation in education the topic might be "student achievement," or "educational attainment," or some other topics. The topic or topic(s) that one starts with are discovered rather idiosyncratically. There is really no general rule. It all depends on what strikes one's fancy and whether or not it bears on the subject matter.

Doctoral students at the initial stages of their programs may not yet have a topic or something that strikes them as interesting. No problem. This just means that they need to read a bit in the field to get some ideas. The first task, in this case, is to find out what journals are the most important in the field and begin to peruse the most recent issues, working backward in time, paying attention to the "things" that the authors are talking about. Students should jot down words or phrases in a notebook or on a computer.

If they do not know what journals are in their field or at least which are the most important, there are two things that students can do. First, they can ask their professor. Second, they can find out what the professional associations are in their field and see what they publish. There are other sources, but these will be covered in more detail in the chapter on how to do the literature review. For the moment, the focus will be on the first—and most important—chapter, the problem statement where students often struggle to figure out what it is they want to know and why it is worth knowing.

It is helpful if the student has a personal and practical reason for wanting to know something. Alan Bloom, a professor at the University of Chicago, has said that all real knowledge begins with a "felt need." He said this in the context that much of what we learn we learn because we must and not because we want to, we learn because someone else told us we have to know it and not because WE feel any need to know it—feel, not think. When it comes to being motivated about something, particularly writing a dissertation, how one FEELS about a topic is important. Authentic interest is important.

So, whatever topic students choose to work on for a dissertation, it should be one that they have a "felt need" to know about. Otherwise, they are asking for trouble and putting themselves at risk of being either an All But Dissertation (ABD) or having to work twice or three times as hard to get the dissertation written.

Having said this, however, it is also important to note that while genuine interest in a topic is important, it is not enough. Students must have more than a personal and practical reason for wanting to study something. They must also have a theoretical reason.

Chapter 7

Problem Statement

Recall that the commonsense question for this chapter is: *What do I want to know and why is it worth knowing?* The purpose of this chapter is to show how to develop a problem statement using one or the other of the two topics as examples—educational attainment and student achievement. Before doing this, however, it might be helpful to recall the commonsense question that the problem-statement chapter is supposed to address. This question is: What do I want to know and why is it worth knowing?

The "problem," in its simplest form, is a general question, a primary question that takes the form of an interrogative statement that captures the phenomenon of interest. The "phenomenon of interest" is the thing that the student happens to be interested in. In the examples used here the things or phenomena are 1) educational attainment, and 2) student achievement. Briefly put, then, *in its simplest form a problem statement is just a question about the thing or topic that the student wants to learn more about.*

Depending upon what the doctoral student wants to know about the thing in which they are interested, the primary question can be formulated in various ways. For example, in the case of educational attainment, the problem statement might be *initially* formulated as follows: Why does educational attainment vary (from one person to the next)? However, upon reflection and from reading, the doctoral student may want to develop this question or reformulate it as discussed in chapter 6. This reformulation or development of the question could take the following form: Is there a relationship between parents' educational attainment and that of their children?

A similar thought process would apply to student achievement. The initial question might be: "What influences student achievement?" However, upon reflection and further reading, the doctoral student may develop this question. As discussed in chapter 6, this reformulation might result in this question: "Is there a relationship between academic self-efficacy and student achievement?"

Doctoral students are apt to find that they reformulate their research questions numerous times as they learn more about the thing they are studying. This is normal. But whatever formulation they finally settle on, in the initial stages of their research they need at least a rough idea of the primary question. This is important because it enables the student to say what it is they want to know. Without at least some initial idea of what they want to know, students will have little idea of where to look. Everything will be relevant. They will find themselves having to "swim" in a veritable ocean of literature and at some point they will inevitably become exhausted and give up. Everything in the dissertation depends on the articulation of the primary phenomenon and the question about it that is to be investigated, even if the initial articulation is only a temporary starting point.[1]

For example, having little idea of their primary question or what it is they want to know, students will be unable to develop a research design, to say what data they will need to collect or what instruments they will use to collect it. Nor will they be able to say how they will analyze the data once they have it. To repeat, the primary research question drives everything else in the dissertation and articulating it, at least in a provisional way, is the first and most important intellectual work that a doctoral student has to do.

While the primary question is the most important part of the problem statement, it needs to be accompanied by at least three other parts. A decent problem statement, then, contains at least the following four sections:

1. Primary question.
2. Rationale or justification of the question.
3. Limitations and delimitations of the research.
4. Key terms and their definitions.

Some researchers may also include in the problem-statement chapter their research hypotheses, a practice more often associated with dissertations that employ a quantitative methodology. There may even be one or two additional sections but the four listed above are among the most important. A word about each may be helpful.

RATIONALE OR JUSTIFICATION OF THE PRIMARY QUESTION

Example: Educational Attainment

Recall again that the commonsense question behind the problem statement: "What do I want to know and why is it worth knowing?" The justification section answers the second part of this question. It consists of one or more reasons why the question is important, and why it is deserving of the student's time and energy to investigate and the committee members' time to read.

In general, justifications of the research question can be of two types: *practical* and *theoretical*. A practical justification of educational attainment, for example, would be related to the goals and missions of higher education institutions. Colleges and universities have as one of their goals enabling students to successfully complete their degree programs. So, given this goal, a practical reason to study educational attainment would be to ascertain the factors that contribute to and impede completion of degree programs, that is, educational attainment.

For example, Leigh McAllen and Helen Johnson found that college faculty can help first generation college students' by "imparting intellectual capital and institutional resources critical to navigating the higher education environment."[2] McAllen and Johnson, therefore, can justify their study on the grounds that knowing what role faculty can play in the success of first-generation college students can help college administrators develop programs to make faculty more aware of what they can do to enable student success. This is a "practical" reason or justification for doing the research, that is, examining the factors that influence educational attainment, particularly that of first-generation students.

A good example of a more "theoretical" justification of the study of educational attainment can be found in a study done by Daniel Ameida and colleagues who compared the effects of "grit" and social capital on first-generation college students' success.[3] In this case, the authors are in effect testing two theories, one having to do with grit and the other with social capital. The general question they investigate is which of the two phenomena seems to have the most effect on college student success. In their study they find that social capital is more important than grit.

The practical question that the study by McAllen and Johnson addresses is of the following sort: "What can college faculty and administration do to improve the experience of first-generation college students?" This question relates to the primary practical question—"What is to be done?" The study by Ameida and colleagues, on the other hand, highlights the theoretical question: "Does a thing exist or what is the case (with the comparative effects of grit vs. social capital on first-generation student success)?" This is not to say that the study by Ameida and colleagues has no practical implications. It is rather simply to emphasize the distinction between practical and theoretical motivations and justifications for carrying out a research project. Each of these studies, in fact, can be and are justified on BOTH practical and theoretical grounds.

Example: Student Achievement

Another example of a theoretical reason to study student achievement can be found in Anathi Lubisi and Fhulu Nekhwevha's article that applies Pierre Bourdieu's cultural reproduction theory to a study of the effects of family background on student achievement or "academic performance."[4] Bourdieu's theory deals with how the social order, particularly social classes, are perpetuated across generations. The study's findings concluded that socioeconomic status of parents/guardians had an impact on the academic performance of grade 12 learners.

An example of a study in which both theoretical and practical significance can be easily seen is Delores Cormier-Zenon's dissertation on the question of whether parents' expectations can compensate for the negative effects of low birth weight on their child's academic achievement.[5] Many children are born prematurely, often in the seventh or eighth month of gestation, or even earlier. Nervous systems of children born early often have not fully developed. Accordingly, they are at risk of various cognitive and neural problems that can affect academic achievement when they reach school age.

Cormier-Zenon found that some of the negative effects of low birth weight can be overcome by parents who have high expectations for their child's development. This is because parents with high expectations tend to do things that stimulate their child's development. They might, for example, read aloud to them, or spend more time playing and interacting with them than parents with low expectations might. Her study was theoretically significant because it supported and was consistent with an extensive body of research on the effects of high expectations for learning. Just as teachers' expectations can affect achievement in the classroom, parents' expectations can make a difference at home, and with very young children. Parents are able do something to compensate for the negative effects that low birth weight has on cognitive development of their children.

Cormier-Zenon's study was also theoretically significant because she used a national data set, the Pre-Elementary Education Longitudinal Study (PEELS) data. These data made her findings more robust because they could be generalized to the US population as a whole.

In addition to its theoretical significance, Cormier-Zenon's study had practical significance. It was practically significant because it suggested to parents with low-birth-weight children that their expectations could make a difference, There were things they could do to counteract the negative effects on their child of being born prematurely. It also held practical significance for how schools could provide information to parents about this correlation.

So, summing up to this point, after stating the main research question, preferably in interrogative form, doctoral students should move to the justification of the question. They can do this simply by beginning their justification paragraphs with a straightforward phrase such as: "This question is important because . . . " and "Another reason this question is important is that . . . " Phrases such as these may seem elementary and perhaps they are. But they also happen to have the virtue of clarity.

SECONDARY QUESTIONS

Every primary question entails secondary questions, questions that arise as one considers and reflects on the primary question. A number of these secondary questions will be questions of meaning. Consider, again, for example, the question of why educational attainment varies from one person to the next. A secondary question associated with this primary question is: "What does 'educational attainment' mean?" This and other questions of meaning can be dealt with in the "key terms" section of the problem statement.

DEFINITION OF KEY TERMS

Let us suppose that the primary question is a simple descriptive question such as the following: *What is the average educational attainment level for Americans and how has this average changed over time?* Now, one secondary question that this primary question immediately brings to mind is: *What do we mean by "educational attainment"?* Before one can say what the average educational attainment level of Americans is, it is necessary to say what is meant by the term "educational attainment." So, the student has to address a secondary question, in this case one of meaning and definition of a key term, before they can address the primary question.

Now, questions of definition or meaning can be addressed in two ways. Students can give the definition of "educational attainment" in the key-terms section of the problem statement. They may also wish to give a short definition of it in the text by way of helping the reader to understand the primary question. For example, after posing the primary question, a student might write: "This study of the average number of years of formal schooling Americans have had is important because . . . "

As students begins to read the literature related to the above example, they will likely try different ways of formulating the question. They might, for example, ask: *What is the average level of educational attainment of Americans and how has it changed over time?* Or, they might state it as follows: *How has the educational attainment level of American changed over time?*

Either formulation would work but the point is that as students get more familiar with the literature related to the question, they will likely discover the terms or "constructs" that other researchers are using and revise their thinking about and formulation of the primary question accordingly. This is a typical occurrence in the dissertation process. The initial formulation of an overarching or primary question is usually rough and approximate and has to be refined as the research progresses.

As students begin to learn more about the things they are interested in—educational attainment, in our example—and the other things to which it is related but yet somehow different, they become more discriminating and sensitive to subtle differences. The "mind's eye" becomes more developed and vision sharpened, and they are able to make fine discriminations that they were not able to do before. This, in fact, is one of the main effects of doctoral program training. It conditions one to see aspects of the world that before the training went unnoticed.

Another secondary question that arises from the primary question in the educational-attainment example has to do with the length of the period over which the average level of education for Americans is to be studied. Does the student wish to compare 2019 with, say, the year 2000 or 1990, 1980, or some prior year? What criteria should be used to decide this? Also, when some particular range of years is finally settled on, why was this period chosen and not some other?

Not surprisingly, these and related questions are often decided, at least in part, by how much data is available or attainable that bears on the primary question. For example, most social scientists and social science students know that they can find the answers to the questions about the educational attainment of Americans in the General Social Survey (GSS). As previously noted, this almost-annual survey of Americans goes back to 1972. So, it is possible to study educational attainment in American over the past five decades.

The point here, however, is that whatever primary question one chooses to study, it will entail one or more secondary questions that also have to be addressed in the course of trying to answer the primary question. A number of these secondary questions will be questions of meaning or questions of definition related to the key terms used in the study.

Another example of how dissertations not only involve a general question but secondary questions involving key terms can be seen in Jason Fountain's study of Americans' work values. Fountain posed the following general question: "Do different generations of Americans have different work values?"[6]

To address this overarching question, Fountain had to ask a more specific question about the meaning of work values, namely, "What are work values?" For him, "work values" was a key term that he had to define before he could address the question of whether or not different generations of Americans hold different work values.

To define "work values," Fountain reviewed literature to see what others before him had done on the topic. In so doing, he was addressing the commonsense questions associated with the literature review: "Who else besides me has been interested in the topic and question I'm interested in? What did they find out? What did they do to find out?"

Perusal of the literature soon led him to J. M. Twenge's theory of generational differences in work attitudes.[7] Twenge, he discovered, had classified work values into different types: "work ethic," "centrality" or importance of work, "altruism," and "intrinsic/extrinsic" values. He decided to adopt Twenge's classification and his theory.

In adopting Twenge's theory of work values, Fountain chose a common strategy used by doctoral students: Use someone else's theory instead of developing one's own. This strategy will be discussed in more detail in the next chapter on the literature review. The strategy to use or "test" someone else's theory solves a number of problems, one of which has to do with developing a conceptual framework. By testing Twenge's theory, Fountain did not have to develop a theory of generational differences of work values on his own but could instead use one already in the literature. This strategy not only assured him that his work would be within the mainstream of ongoing research on the topic but also saved him valuable research time.

Using Twenge's theory, Fountain raised a number of questions that were related to his more general, overarching question: "Do different generations of Americans differ in their views of work ethic, work centrality and leisure values?" Do different generations of Americans differ in their views of altruistic values? Do they differ in their intrinsic/extrinsic values?" and so on.

Fountain was also able to test an existing theory because he was able to access GSS data, one of the federal government's many online data sets. As already noted, the GSS was developed and funded by the National Science Foundation. More will be said about this particular data set and the more general issue of using existing or "archival" data in the chapter on methodology. At this point let it suffice to say that students using a survey research methodology have available to them online, 24/7, a number of high-quality data sets that have been put together by various government agencies.

If they can locate one of these data sources, especially one as reliable and accessible as the GSS, doctoral students will likely be able to shorten their doctoral program by at least a semester if not a year or more. This is because they will not have to do the first two steps of survey research: research design and data collection. They can, instead, devote their time to the third step of analyzing the data already made available to them. But more will be said on this point in due course.

But these details aside, the main point is that Fountain did have an overarching or primary question that he could come back to again and again to remind himself of what his study was about. The primary question served as a compass that kept him on track as he sifted through the dozens of studies on his topic.

LIMITATIONS AND DELIMITATIONS OF THE STUDY

It is sometimes the case that the student would like to include something in the study for which there is little information or no data available. This situation constitutes a "limitation" of the study. In general, a limitation is something that the researcher would like to do or that, in the best of all possible worlds, the study would include but the thing desired is not available or attainable. The student should not ignore these situations but admit them as limitations to the study.

A related but different issue concerns delimitations of the study. In this case, the data may be available but the student does not wish to include them in the study. In an analysis of the educational attainment of Americans, for example, the doctoral student may have data on the regions of the country in which each case or individual in their sample population lives but may not wish to include this information, perhaps because they think it is not directly related to the primary question being addressed. This decision to exclude a variable from the study constitutes a delimitation of the study.

NOTES

1. Qualitative research is more inductive in this regard. The primary research question is allowed to be more emergent than articulated early in the research. On this point see Barney Glaser and Anselm Strauss' *The Discovery of Grounded Theory* (New York: Routledge, 1999).

2. Leigh McCallen and Helen Johnson, "The Role of Institutional Agents in Promoting Higher Education Success among First-Generation College Students at a Public Urban University," *Journal of Diversity in Higher Education* 13, no. 4 (2020): 320–32.

3. Daniel Almeida, Andrew M. Byrne, Rachel M. Smith, and Saul Ruiz, "How Relevant Is Grit? The Importance of Social Capital in First-Generation College Students Academic Success," *Journal of College Student Retention: Research, Theory & Practice* 23, no. 3 (2021): 539–59.

4. Anathi Lubisi and Fhulu Nekhwevha, "Effects of Family Background Performance of Grade 12 Learners," *International Journal of Social Science Research and Review* 7, no. 1 (2024): 270–77.

5. Dolores E. Cormier-Zenon, "Can Parental Expectations Compensate for the Negative Effects of Low Birth Weight on Academic Achievement: A Cross-Sectional Analysis of the National PEELS Data" (EdD diss., the University of Louisiana at Lafayette, 2012).

6. See Jason M. Fountain, "Differences in Generational Work Values in America and Their Implications for Educational Leadership: A Longitudinal Test of Twenge's Model" (EdD diss., the University of Louisiana at Lafayette, 2014), 1.

7. J. M. Twenge, "A Review of the Empirical Evidence on Generational Differences in Work Attitudes," *Journal of Business Psychology* 25 (2010): 201–10.

Chapter 8

Literature Review and Conceptual Framework

Recall the commonsense questions that inform and structure the literature review: Who else besides me has wanted to know what I want to know or something like I want to know? What did they find out and what did they do to find out? Given what I have learned from the literature on this question, what is my best guess about what I am going to find out when I analyze the data?

A literature review is a report about the most important work that has already been done on a question; as the commonsense question suggests, it attempts to summarize what is already known about a thing. It "provides a means of grounding your research and explaining its relevance."[1]

For example, a literature review on educational attainment in the United States could be expected to summarize what is already known about how much formal schooling Americans have attained to date, to say what the average level of educational attainment is for different groups, and how and why this average differs or varies according to race, class, gender, and other variables. The reader of such a literature review could expect to be told these things by way of a discussion of the most important or salient research studies on the topic. Along the way, the reader might also find it useful to know how the studies were conducted, their design, and their source of data. A review, in short, should bring the reader "up to speed" on the research being done on a topic and its associated questions.

A review of what has already been discovered about the topic in question sets up the conceptual framework. Much ink has been spilled about the nature of conceptual frameworks and theory, and it is not necessary here to get into the details of all the epistemological discussions surrounding the debate on what a conceptual framework is. The approach taken here is straightforward and consistent with the assumption that research in general and theorizing in particular come down to addressing a set of questions about some thing in which the student happens to have an interest, a thing the understanding of which also happens to be of interest to a broader research community. From this perspective, developing a conceptual framework or a theory about how a thing works is mainly a process of answering one or more of the theoretical questions discussed in chapter 5.

THE LITERATURE REVIEW AS DISCOVERY

Every doctoral student should have as their primary goal the writing and defense of a good—not a perfect—dissertation. When it comes to doing dissertations, the goal of perfection, however noble it may seem, can turn out to be an obstacle. Most students find it more productive to strive for a good rather than perfect piece of work. With this more modest standard, the quality of what they finally end up with often turns out to be surprisingly better than they imagined it might be. The stress and strains of doing a dissertation do not need to be strengthened by the pursuit of an ideal which, in this context, can result in writer's block. Better to approach the task with a workman-like attitude.

Approached in a workman-like fashion, the literature review can become a stress-reducing activity. The student should look upon the literature review as a chance to survey how scholars in their field are thinking about the very thing or things in which they themselves are interested. Most students come to a doctoral program with one or two "topics" in mind. An examination of what has been done on their topic will likely introduce them to new ways of thinking about it or even point them in a related but different direction altogether. The literature review should be viewed as an opportunity for discovery.

SOURCES

Preliminary sources. A useful approach to reviewing literature has been suggested by Meredith Gall and coauthors.[2] With at least a rough idea of the general topic and question in mind, the first step they suggest is to identify and search the preliminary sources. These are essentially lists of various literatures. Most preliminary sources are now online. They include in education, for example, Education Abstracts and ERIC. In sociology, there is Sociological Abstracts. Political science has the Political Science Index. More generally, most academic libraries enable students to access Academic Search Complete, EBSCO, JSTOR, and the like. Also, of course, there is Google Scholar. These and other preliminary sources should be the first places students go to get a sense of what has been done on their topic/research question.

Secondary sources. A search of preliminary sources will likely turn up documents written by authors who did not have firsthand knowledge or make direct observations of the phenomena under investigation but instead report on the results or findings of those who did have such knowledge. These are secondary sources. Some secondary sources, such as reviews of the literature, can be particularly useful for their summaries and interpretations of the studies that have been done on a topic/question. Some important secondary sources in education are Review of Research in Education and Review of Educational Research.

Primary sources. Primary sources are reports done by those who have done firsthand observations of events. These could be original articles in academic journals, books, government reports, and the like. Primary sources typically advance empirical, theoretical, and methodological understanding. They are the subject matter of secondary sources such as literature reviews. In education, for example, primary sources are found in the *American Educational Research Journal*. In sociology, a journal publishing primary source articles is the *American Sociological Review*. In political science, it is the *American Political Science Review*. Each major discipline usually has a flagship journal in which original articles can be found.

CONCEPTUAL/THEORETICAL FRAMEWORK

Questions about what a theory is and how or whether it differs from a conceptual framework are matters taken up in a serious way by philosophers of science. Students wishing to pursue these and related questions in some depth might want to start by consulting the *Stanford Encyclopedia of Philosophy*. This would probably be a better place to begin an inquiry into the nature of theory than the myriad of articles and even books on the subject done by social scientists and educational theorists, many of whom simply lack the philosophical training to deal with the subject adequately.

For present purposes, a pragmatic approach will be taken to address the question of what a conceptual or theoretical framework should consist of for dissertation work. With this approach, the conceptual or theoretical framework in the dissertation should be guided by one or more of the theoretical questions previously discussed. Most theoretical frameworks deal with the two theoretical questions dealing with causes and effects.

Recall from the previous discussion that the theoretical question related to causes is: Why does a thing exist or vary? In this case the researcher is interested in the factors or variables that can explain why the thing of interest exists or varies. Put in terms of a more quantitative methodology, the researcher wants to know what independent or criterion variables influence or affect the dependent variable of interest. Figure 8.1 illustrates the logic of a framework in which the X variables are presumed to influence the variation in the Y, dependent variable.

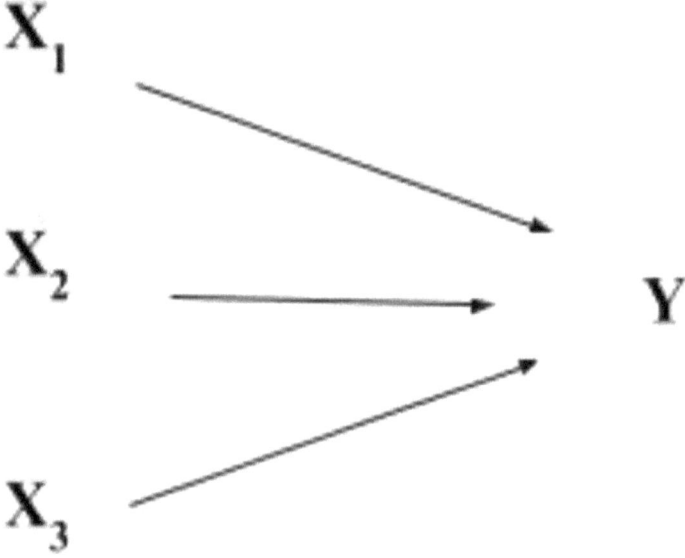

Figure 8.1: Model of the influence of independent variables, X1-3, on dependent variable, Y

An example of a substantive application of this logic would be the phenomenon of educational attainment. In terms of the model in 8.1, educational attainment would be the dependent or Y variable. Factors that influence educational attainment might include father's and mother's educational attainment and family income at age sixteen. Plugging these constructs into the figure results in figure 8.2

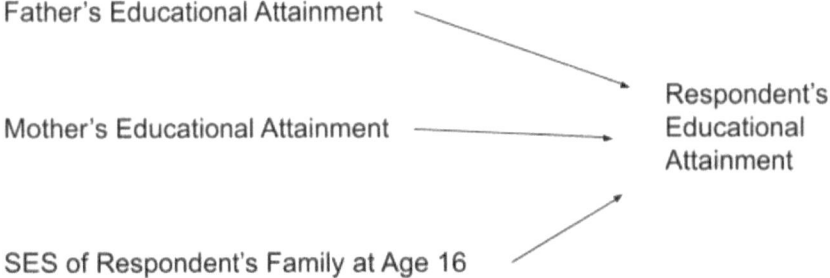

Figure 8.2: Model of educational attainment and factors hypothesized to influence it

Alternatively, the researcher might be interested in the consequences or effects of a particular phenomenon. The logic of relationships between variables in this case is expressed in figure 8.3

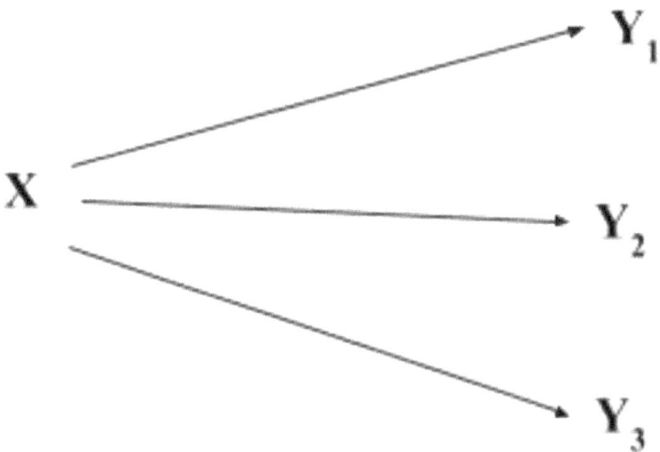

Figure 8.3: Model of influence of independent variable X on dependent variables Y1-3

Figure 8.4 shows the application of this logical model with specific constructs using, again, educational attainment as an example.

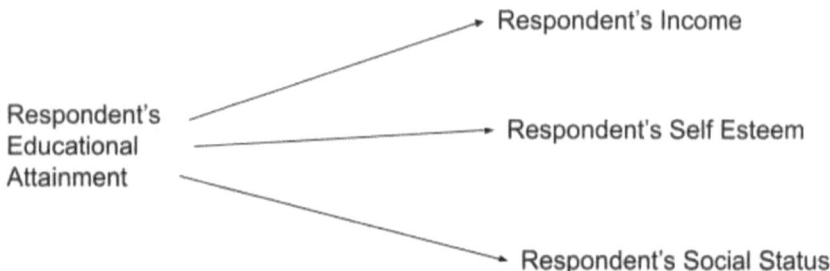

Figure 8.4: Model of educational attainment and the factors it might be hypothesized to influence

A conceptual or theoretical framework in a dissertation, then, is a model of the relationship between and among constructs. Most conceptual frameworks address the two theoretical questions having to do with cause and effect. The question of what causes a thing to exist or vary is illustrated in figures 8.1 and 8.2, and the question of what the consequences of a thing are is illustrated in figures 8.3 and 8.4.

When it comes to developing a conceptual or theoretical framework, doctoral students often look to the literature and previous studies done on or around their topic. In most cases, they use a framework developed by other scholars. They may use the framework as it is and thus essentially do a replication study, or they may modify the framework slightly with an additional or other variable and use their own data to test it.

The foregoing discussion assumes a quantitative methodological approach. A qualitative methodology would not likely involve hypothesis and model development as has just been described. A grounded-theory approach, in fact, might not develop a conceptual framework until the data have been collected and analyzed. But whether students choose to take a quantitative or qualitative approach in their studies, the theoretical questions and the models they suggest can be used to organize their thoughts on a topic.

NOTES

1. Hilary Burgess, Sandy Sieminski, and Lori Arthur, *Achieving Your Doctorate in Education* (Thousand Oaks, CA: Sage, 2006), 19.

2. See Meredith D. Gall, Joyce P. Gall, and Walter Borg, *Educational Research: An Introduction*, 8th ed. (Boston: Pearson, 2007), 95–122.

Chapter 9

Methodology

The commonsense question that guides this chapter is: Given what I want to know about, and what others before me have found out about it, and what they did to find out, what am I going to do to find out what I want to know?

With the traditional five-chapter dissertation structure, the "methodology" discussion occurs in chapter 3. Methodology chapters in education dissertations typically have the following parts or sections: introduction, research design, participants, data-collection procedures, data-analysis procedures, instrumentation, reliability and validity, IRB statement, limitations and delimitations, and summary. A word about each of these sections follows.

INTRODUCING THE CHAPTER

The introduction section to the methodology chapter should restate the general purpose/question that the study is attempting to answer. For example, the researcher might write, "The purpose of this study is to examine the relationship between parents' educational attainment and that of their children." Or, "As stated at the outset, the investigation of this relationship is important because . . . " A statement of this type should help the reader make sense of the choice of the research design and other sections of the chapter.

RESEARCH DESIGNS

Broadly speaking, research designs tend to involve quantitative, qualitative, or mixed methods. Quantitative designs, in turn, tend to be either *experimental* or *nonexperimental*.

Experimental Designs

With the experimental design, the researcher manipulates the variables being studied. For example, if one wished to study educational attainment with an experimental design, the researchers would have to manipulate educational attainment. They would, for example, have to "give" some people more formal schooling than others and let some time pass to see what difference it made on, say, individuals' income. This would not only make for a long and complicated study but more importantly, it would be unethical to deliberately deprive some of formal schooling while enabling others to receive it just to find out whether those who got more education earned more money. Accordingly, educational attainment needs to be studied with a nonexperimental design.

Nonexperimental Designs

The logic of a *nonexperimental* design is that the events have already occurred and are merely being observed. So, in the case of educational attainment, the task is not, as with the experimental design, to "give" some people more education than others, but rather to compare individuals with different amounts of educational attainment to see if, say, how much their incomes might vary.

THE POST-HOC-CAUSAL-COMPARATIVE DESIGN

A commonly used design in survey data analysis, and one that would utilize the GSS data to study educational attainment, is the "post-hoc-causal-comparative design." It is "post-hoc" meaning it is after the fact . . . the fact being the amount of education individuals have attained. It is causal because the researcher is hypothesizing that educational attainment causes or influences something else, in this example, personal income. It is comparative because the researcher is interested in comparing people with less education with people who have more, thinking that those who have more will have more income than those who have less.

CORRELATIONAL RESEARCH DESIGNS

A researcher might choose to use a correlational research design when they are interested in finding out whether a relationship may exist between variables even if the relationship is not hypothesized to be causal. Perhaps, for example, the researcher wishes to know whether there is a correlation between the size of an institution of higher education and the four-year graduation rate of its undergraduate population. This knowledge might be sought without the belief that the size of the institution in any way "causes" the graduation rate.

With both the causal-comparative and correlational designs it should be noted that any proposition to the effect that one thing "causes" another is grounded in conceptual and theoretical considerations and not empirical evidence. The usual phrase employed to make this point is that "correlation does not mean causation."

On the topic of survey research, doctoral students might find the data they need to do their studies in one of the numerous "archival" data sets that have been developed by various government agencies and made available to the public online. For doctoral students in education or the social sciences, two in particular might prove helpful.

One is managed by the Institute for Education Sciences (IES), which can be accessed at https://ies.ed.gov/. As its website explains, IES is "the nation's leading source for rigorous, independent education research, evaluation and statistics." Like many other government agencies, IES makes available data sets that researchers can use to do their work. As of this writing, IES has data available from no less than twenty-one surveys. For doctoral students in education, these data are an excellent source for their dissertation work.

Another excellent archival data is the General Social Survey or GSS. Funded by the National Science Foundation and administered by the University of Chicago's National Opinion Research Center, the GSS is one of the most reliable and often-used data sets in the social sciences. It is available on various websites but one of the most accessible and easiest to use is that provided by the University of California at Berkeley, which can be accessed at http://sda.berkeley.edu/.

Doctoral students interested in doing research with national data on important topics of the day have these and other large, reliable, and clean data sets at their disposal 24/7. They need not worry about the quality of these data, for millions of dollars have been invested and hundreds of expert researchers in education and the social sciences have been involved in the design of the research and collection of the information behind them. These data sets are among the best available on American education and Americans in general. Researchers the world over use them and publish the results of their analyses in some of the most prestigious educational and social science research journals. Graduate students who are interested in and willing to use these archives can explore and investigate literally hundreds of research questions.

Given the availability of excellent data in archives such these, one would think that doctoral students would flock to them for their dissertation work but for a number of reasons they do not. One reason is probably that there still lingers in doctoral programs the old-fashioned idea that students should always collect their own data because it gives them firsthand experience with research design and data-collection problems and techniques, knowledge and skills that they will need when they do additional research.

There is some truth to the view that students can benefit from designing their own research and collecting their own data but perhaps not as much as adherents to this view suppose. Firsthand research design and data collection does give students practice in research design and data collection. But the downside is that the data they collect and analyze is usually quite local in its application, and the ability to generalize research findings to a broader universe is quite limited. Students could just easily examine a research topic/question at the national level using one of these large data sets and then see whether what they find at the national level holds good for a smaller geographical area.

Some students start out with a commitment to a particular methodology. When they are asked, for example, what their study is about they may reply that they plan to do a survey of a particular group of people. This kind of reply, while common, indicates a lack of understanding of the general point of a dissertation and perhaps even of the central question they need to address. A more intelligent response to the question of what their research is about would be one in which they say what their topic of interest is what they want to know about it. The student should acquire the habit of making a response like this in no more than a sentence or two, not only because that is all most people are interested in hearing but also because it will serve as a reminder to themselves of what they are trying to accomplish.

In addition to a discussion of the research design to be used in the study, other elements in the methodology chapter will include a description of the data and its source, and a discussion of Institutional Review Board (IRB) requirements and how they were met. If a quantitative study, also included will be the names, definitions, and measures of key variables in the study as well as a description of the statistical techniques used to analyze the data.

For a more detailed discussion of the contents of the methodology chapter of the dissertation, students should consult *Educational Research: An Introduction* by Meredith Gall and colleagues or a similar text.[1]

DATA SOURCE AND SAMPLING

As already noted in earlier chapters, this book focuses on two phenomena or variables: educational attainment and student achievement. The government data set used here to examine educational attainment is the General Social Survey or GSS. In the "Data Source" section of the Methodology chapter the student would give information about the the GSS data, how it was collected, the sampling procedure used, and the like. This information is readily available on the main website of the National Opinion Research Center, which administers and maintains the GSS.[2] What follows is an example of a description of the GSS data source taken from a dissertation done by Dr. Chun Lau:[3]

> To operationalize this design and investigate this research question, data from the nationally representative General Social Survey (GSS), which is administered by the National Opinion Research Center (NORC), were utilized. The GSS is a sociological survey program conducted by the National Opinion Research Center (NORC) across U.S. household populations that employs a full-probability, cluster-randomized, and single-interview methodology designed to monitor changes in both social characteristics and attitudes currently being conducted in the United States (Smith, Marsden, Hout, & Kim, 2011). The survey used a multiple stage selection process to gather data from a representative sample (Smith et al., 2011, p. 2879). The first stage was selecting a sample from the Office of Management and Budget defined counties and metropolitan areas, called "consolidated statistical areas," based on area population (Smith et al., 2011, p. 2879). These units were sampled in proportions representative of the U.S. population urban-rural demographics (Smith et al., 2011, p. 2879).
>
> Between 1972 and 1994, NORC administered the survey every year in February, March, and April, except in 1979, 1981, and 1992. Beginning in 1994, the survey frequency changed to every other year. Among the topics covered are civil liberties, crime and violence, intergroup tolerance, morality, national spending priorities, psychological well-being, social mobility, and stress and traumatic events. The GSS is the single best source for sociological and attitudinal trend data covering the United States. (GSS Website)
>
> This study draws on the GSS 1972–2018 Cross-Sectional Cumulative Data file (Release 1, March 2019), which contains all data points from 1972 to 2018. The initial data set for this study was limited to surveys conducted in 2012 (N = 7,033 cases). The data includes 1 independent variables, 3 controlling variables, and a dependent variable.
>
> With a cumulative database of 64,814 interviews of adult people at least 18 years of age from 1972–2018, the GSS allows for a sample of Americans' political participation to be drawn at different time periods. This dissertation focuses on the time period of 2012. In order to better understand the changes and trends in the political participation of Americans with low levels of education versus their highly educated counterparts, logistic regression modeling was conducted to explore how the independent variable impact political participation.

If the student chooses not use a government-developed data set, such as the GSS or NAEP with their extensive websites, he or she should include a copy of their data collection instrument—survey or other form—in an appendix and refer to it in this section of the chapter.

THE NULL HYPOTHESES, AND TYPE I AND II ERRORS

Quantitative research often involves hypothesis testing. The researcher, for example, may wish to test an hypothesis about the relationship between educational attainment and political participation as Chun Lau did in his dissertation. The idea might be that the more formal education a person has, the more likely they are to vote. There may be various reasons for this. Some research indicates that education makes one feel more responsible for getting involved in civic affairs and this sense of responsibility may prompt one to vote. Higher education also tends to be associated with an interest in being involved in decisions that affect the public's business such as road construction and repairs, schools, hospitals, the police and fire departments and other municipal business. This interest translates into voting local public officials. For these and other reasons, the researcher may believe that there is a relationship between educational attainment and political participation.

Wanting to test an hypothesis about the relationship between educational attainment and political participation, the researcher can test either a directional or *null* hypothesis. The null hypothesis for the relationship between educational attainment and political participation would read: "There is no relationship between educational attainment and political participation." One can test this hypothesis using a contingency table. Table 9.1 shows a contingency table of the relationship between educational attainment and voting (political participation) using data from the 2016 General Social Survey 2020.[4]

Focusing on the table's far right column total, we see that the sample consists of a total of 5,652 adult Americans. Now, looking at the column for those respondents with less than a high school education we can see that a total of 373 respondents reported having less than a high school education, and of these 373, 188 or 50 percent said they voted in the 2016 election. By comparison, 848 or 90 percent of respondents who reported having a graduate degree said that they voted in the 2016 election. So, respondents with a graduate degree were 40 percentage points (90–50) more likely than those with less than a high school diploma to vote. These data indicate that there is a relationship between educational attainment and political participation. The greater the educational attainment, the more likely one is to vote. The "p" value is .00 indicating that this relationship is statistically significant. Therefore, we should reject the null hypothesis.

Now, let us suppose that for some reason, the sample above of 5,652 Americans was incorrectly drawn, that is, that it was not randomly drawn, and that what we see in the table does not actually reflect the distribution of educational attainment and political participation in the population as

Table 9.1 Educational Attainment by Voting in US Presidential Election 2016

Degree Earned

Voted?	Less Than High School	High School	Junior College	College	Graduate	TOTALS
Yes	50%	72%	80%	87%	90%	78%
	(188)	(1,728)	(415)	(1,223)	(848)	(4,492)
No	50	28	20	13	10	22
	(185)	(688)	(106)	(181)	(90)	(1,250)
TOTAL	100%	100%	100%	1100%	100%	100%
	(373)	(2,416)	(521)	(1,404)	(938)	5,652
$p = .00$						

Source: Survey Documentation and Analysis, University of California–Berkeley, https://sda.berkeley.edu/archive.htm

a whole, the population from which the sample was drawn, which, in the case of the GSS, is all noninstitutionalized Americans age eighteen or older. In rejecting the null hypothesis, therefore, we could be making an error. The null hypothesis says that there is no relationship. The 40-point percentage difference we see in the table between the least and the most educated Americans is not the case with the actual population. The error we would be making in rejecting the null hypothesis in this case would be a Type I error. We reject the null hypothesis when we should not have.

Now, here's the question: How does one know whether to reject the null hypothesis? The answer to this question involves the p value. The p value indicates the probability of committing a Type I error, that is, of rejecting the null hypothesis when it should not be rejected. Statisticians have put their heads together and decided that, in cases like the one we are considering here, if we see a p values equal to or less than .05 we can be relatively confident that we will not commit a Type I error in rejecting the null hypothesis. This is because with a p value of .05 or less we have a 1 in 20 chance of committing a Type I error and these are pretty good odds.

In the case of table 9.1 we see that the p value is even less, considerably less than the .05 cut off. In fact, the p value for this table is .00, which means that we probably have less than 1 out of a 1,000 chance of committing a Type I error. Accordingly, we can be confident that the 40 percentage point difference we are seeking between the least and most educated Americans approximates what we would see if we were to do the analysis with the entire population instead of with the sample we are using.

So, we commit a Type I error when we reject the null hypothesis when we should not reject it. A Type II error is when we FAIL to reject the null hypothesis and we should have rejected it. Perhaps it would help understand the difference between the two types of errors by providing some examples closer to real life.

Null Hypothesis Example 1: Dr. Null and the Marriage Proposal

Imagine a student is seeking a significant other and that he or she believes they have found him or her. The student and the significant other would like to get married. But the happy couple want to be sure that they are making the right decision. So, they decide to consult Dr. Null on the matter. When they meet with Dr. Null and explain their decision, his response is emphatic: "There is no relationship here! What you think you feel is not real but just temporary. Under no circumstances should you marry! In six months, you will be divorced!" So, what should the couple do? They can either reject Dr. Null's advice (the null hypothesis) and marry. Or they can fail to reject his advice and not go through with the marriage. What kind of mistake or error could they make in either case?

Suppose they reject Dr. Null's advice (the null hypothesis) and go ahead and marry. However, sure enough, it turns out that soon both are miserable and six months later they are divorced. In this case they have, in rejecting Dr. Null's advice, committed a Type I error. They have rejected the null hypothesis when they should not have.

On the other hand, let us suppose that they do not reject Dr. Null's advice. They listen and take to heart what he has told them. They decide not to marry. They break off their relationship, and each person and marries someone else. However, as time passes they realize that they have lost the love of their life. In this case, sadly, they have committed a Type II error: They failed to reject Dr. Null's advice when they should have rejected it.

Obviously, a student wants to avoid both types of error. In either case they end up regretting their decision. The p values help decide what to do. The p value indicates the chances of committing a Type I or II error.

Null Hypothesis Example 2: The Oil Well Venture

Again, imagine this time that a student has worked many years to save up a nest egg that will allow her to just barely retire so that she can finally complete writing her dissertation. Just as she is about to retire, a good friend comes to her with the news that a new technological device has been invented that can find oil, and that it has indicated that there is a huge oil deposit in a plot of land he owns in Texas. If the student invests her savings in his drilling venture she can be fabulously wealthy. Not sure what to do, the student decides to consult Dr. Null on the matter. She asks him whether she should invest in this very promising venture. Dr. Null's response is, of course, predictable. He says, quite emphatically, "No! Do not invest in this venture!

There is no relationship between that device and oil in the ground. There is nothing there!"

If the student rejects Dr. Null's advice and invests her life savings and the oil well turns out to be a dry hole she has committed a Type I error. She has rejected the null hypothesis and should not have. On the other hand, if she fails to reject Dr. Null's advice and does not invest and it turns out to be the gusher of the century, she has committed a Type II error. The point is not to commit any error! If she consults the p value she is likely to avoid doing so.

VARIABLES, DEFINITIONS, AND MEASURES

Whether a student uses the GSS, NAEP, or some other data set for their data source, they should list the variables in their study, as well as their definitions, and their measures. This can be done in a table such as 9.2 which shows the two variables involved in table 9.1 along with their definitions and measures. Note that in table 9.2 the "Measures" include the actual GSS questions asked of the respondents in the survey.

In this section of the Methodology chapter the student should also include the basic frequency information for each of the variables in the study. These can be included in either the text or in an Appendix.

STATISTICAL ANALYSIS PROCEDURES

In this section of the Methodology chapter, the student should describe the statistical procedures to be used to analyze the data.

Table 9.2 Variables, Definitions, and Measures

Variable Name	Definitions	Measures (GSS)
Educational Attainment	The amount of formal schooling attained	What is the highest grade in elementary school or highschool that you finished and got credit for?
Political Participation in 2016 Presidential Election (name of GSS variable: "Pres16")	How respondent voted in 2016 presidential election.	Did you vote for Clinton or Trump? 1. Clinton 2. Trump 3. Other 4. Didn't vote for president

NOTES

1. Meredith Gall, Joyce Gall, and Walter Borg, *Educational Research: An Introduction* (New York: Sage, 2007).
2. National Opinion Research Center, "The General Social Survey," https://www.norc.org/research/projects/gss.html.
3. See Chun Lau, "Exploring the Relationship between Educational Attainment and Political Participation," adissertation.
4. The University of California–Berkeley, Survey Documentation and Analysis, accessed at https://sda.berkeley.edu/sdaweb/analysis/?dataset=gss22rel2.

Chapter 10

Data Analysis and Discussion

Recall that the commonsense question that guides this chapter: *What did I find out about what I wanted to know?* In this data-analysis chapter of the dissertation the purpose is to find out what one wants to know by looking at data related to the research question.

Example: Educational Attainment and Happiness

The student should begin by reminding the reader of what the primary research question of the study is. Keeping with the example of "educational attainment," suppose that the student wishes to know whether attaining more education makes one happier. The initial paragraph of this chapter should be straightforward. An example might be:

> The purpose of this study is to examine the relationship between educational attainment and happiness. The question investigated is as follows: Do Americans with more formal education tend to be happier than those with less?

Next, the student can remind the reader of the hypothesis to be tested. If the student chooses to go with the null hypothesis in this case, they might write:

> The null hypothesis to be tested is: "There is no relationship between educational attainment and happiness."

However, should the student choose to go with a *directional* hypothesis instead of the null, the wording might go as follows:

> The directional hypothesis to be tested is: "The greater the educational attainment, the greater the happiness."

By making this or something like it the opening paragraph of the data analysis and discussion chapter, the student clearly states at the outset what the whole chapter is about. The reader is told in effect that there will be an analysis of the relationship between two variables. In this example, the variables are the educational attainment and happiness of the survey respondent.

Following this reminder of what the general research question is and the hypothesis to be tested, the student should then move directly into the bivariate analysis. Here, again, a contingency table, as shown in table 10.1 could be used as a start. In this case, the student might write:

> Is there a relationship between educational attainment and happiness? Table 10.1 indicates a small but statistically significant relation. For example, while 69 percent of the 358 respondents with less than a high school education said that they were happy, by comparison, 85 percent of the 485 respondents who reported having a graduate degree said that they were happy. The data indicate, then, that respondents with graduate degrees were 16 percentage points more likely to say that they were happy than respondents with less than a high school education. There appears to be a small but statistically significant relationship between happiness and educational attainment.

Following this introductory bivariate (two-variable) analysis, the student might wish to enter a third variable, say, race. In this case, the wording would then be something like the following:

> Now, is the relationship between educational attainment and happiness indicated in table 10.1 the same for Black and White Americans? In other words, does the relationship change when controlling for race? Tables 10.2 and 10.3 address this question. In table 10.2, 73 percent of Whites with less than a high school education said they were happy. By comparison, 89 percent of those with a graduate education reported being happy. White Americans with the most education were 16 percentage points more likely than Americans with the least education to say they were happy. Now, the data in table 10.2 indicate that the difference between the least and most educated Black Americans is 13 percentage points (71 percent vs. 84 percent), not much different from Whites. So, it appears that the relationship between educational attainment and happiness is very similar for both White and Black Americans.

Example: Students' Efficacy and Reading Achievement

A similar process would apply to the examination of NAEP data. Consider, for example, an analysis of the relationship between student achievement in reading and student reading efficacy, that is, the confidence they have in their reading knowledge and skills.[1] The student might write the following:

> The main research question concerns the relationship between students' reading efficacy and their reading achievement. The hypothesis to be tested can be stated

Table 10.1 Happiness by Educational Attainment (2022)

	Less Than High School	High School	Associate/Junior College	Bachelor's	Graduate	ROW TOTAL
Happy	69% (247)	76% (1,240)	77% (244)	80% (586)	85% (404)	77 (2,721)
Not too Happy	31 (111)	24 (400)	23 (73)	20 (144)	15 (71)	23 (799)
COL TOTAL	100% (358)	100% (1,640)	100% (317)	100% (730)	100% (475)	100% 3,520
Means	1.31	1.24	1.23	1.20	1.15	1.23
Std Devs	.46	.43	.42	.40	.36	.42

Source: Survey Documentation and Analysis, University of California–Berkeley, accessed at: SDA: Survey Documentation and Analysis (berkeley.edu).

Table 10.2 Happiness by Educational Attainment for White Americans (2010–2022)

	Less Than High School	High School	Associate/Junior College	Bachelor's	Graduate	ROW TOTAL
Happy	73% (929)	82% (5,508)	82% (967)	87% (2,742)	89% (1,739)	83 (11,885)
Not too Happy	27 (338)	18 (1,213)	18 (209)	13 (411)	11 (219)	17 (2,390)
COL TOTAL	100% (1,267)	100% (6,721)	100% (1,167)	100% (3,153)	100% (1,958)	100% (14,275)
Means	1.27	1.24	1.18	1.13	1.11	1.17
Std Devs	.44	.43	.38	.34	.32	.37
p = 0.00						

Source: Survey Documentation and Analysis, University of California–Berkeley, accessed at: SDA: Survey Documentation and Analysis (berkeley.edu).

as follows: "The greater the students' reading efficacy, the higher their reading scores." As explained in the methodology chapter, the data to be used to test this hypothesis is from the National Assessment of Educational Progress study.

Now, is there a relationship between student efficacy and reading achievement? Table 10.4 shows the relationship between student efficacy scores and reading achievement scores for fourth graders in the nation's public schools for 2022. The data in the table indicate that there is a relationship. The average score on the NAEP reading test for fourth graders with "low" efficacy was 181. By contrast, the average score for students with "high" efficacy was 235, a 54-point difference. Moreover, significance tests show these differences in scores between the low and high students to be statistically

Table 10.3 Happiness by Educational Attainment for Black Americans (2010–2022)

	Less Than High School	High School	Associate/Junior College	Bachelor's	Graduate	ROW TOTAL
Happy	71% (284)	76% (1,161)	78% (208)	80% (344)	84% (208)	77 (2,205)
Not to Happy	29 (115)	24 (369)	22 (58)	20 (84)	16 (41)	23 (667)
COL TOTAL	100% (399)	100% (1,530)	100% (266)	100% (428)	100% (249)	100% (2,872)
Means	1.29	1.24	1.22	1.20	1.16	1.23
Std Devs	.45	.43	.41	.40	.37	.42

p = 0.00

Source: Survey Documentation and Analysis, University of California–Berkeley, accessed at: SDA: Survey Documentation and Analysis (berkeley.edu).

Table 10.4 Fourth-Grade Reading Scores by Student Reading Efficacy

Year	Jurisdiction	Students' Confidence in Reading Knowledge and Skills	Average Scale Score
2022	National Public	Low	181
		Moderate	209
		High	235

p < 0.00

significant. It appears, then, that the correlation between reading efficacy and reading achievement is moderate to strong and statistically significant.

Having shown the bivariate relationship between efficacy and reading scores, doctoral students may then wish to find out whether the relationship is the same for, say, boys and girls. Accordingly, they would then run the analysis again but controlling for gender. The result is presented in table 10.5 and, with these results, the doctoral student might write:

> While there appears to be a moderate to strong statistically significant relationship between students' efficacy and their reading scores, is this relationship the same for both males and females? Table 10.5 indicates that it is. While the data in the table show that girls tend to score a bit higher than boys on the NAEP reading tests, the difference between the scores of the "low" efficacy boys and the "high" efficacy boys is 234–178 or 56 points. For the girls the difference is 236–186 or 50 points. There is only a 6-point difference between the "effects" of efficacy on boys' scores as compared to the girls.' Efficacy, in other words, correlates with reading scores regardless of gender.

Table 10.5 Fourth-Grade Reading Scores by Student Reading Efficacy by Gender

Year	Jurisdiction		Students' Confidence in Reading Knowledge and Skills		
2022	National Public		Low	Moderate	High
		Male	178	207	234
		Female	186	212	236
$p < 0.00$					

SUMMARY

The student should close out the "Data Analysis" chapter by summing up by restating the research question and/or hypotheses and then follow with the overall results of the analysis. Summing up the educational-attainment-happiness analysis the student might write:

The analysis of the educational-attainment-happiness relationship indicates that educational attainment and happiness are correlated. The more formal schooling Americans have, the more likely they are to report being happy. Moreover, this is the case for both White and Black Americans.

A similar type of summary should work for the efficacy-reading-achievement relationship. In this case, the doctoral student might write:

The analysis indicates that public school fourth-grade students' confidence in their reading knowledge and skills, that is, their reading efficacy, is correlated with their reading scores. This, moreover, appears to be the case for both boys and girls. The relationship does not substantially change when controlling for gender.

NOTE

1. The NAEP question in this case is an aggregate of several questions among two of which are: "Do you think you would be able to do each of the following when reading? Figure out the meaning of a word you don't know by using other words in the text (student-reported)," and "Do you think you would be able to do each of the following when reading? Explain the meaning of something you have read (student-reported)." Based on their answers to these and similar questions, students' efficacy or confidence scores are then rated in three categories: "low," "moderate," and "high" confidence.

Chapter 11

Summary, Conclusions, and Recommendations

Recall that four commonsense questions guide this chapter: *What did I start out wanting to know? What did I find out? So what?* and *What more needs to be done?* As the title of this chapter suggests, in this final chapter of the dissertation, the student is expected to once again remind the reader of what it is they set out to know in the first place, what they found out from their investigation, the theoretical and practical significance of it all, and what more remains to be done.

Example: Educational Attainment and Happiness

Using the example of educational attainment's relationship with happiness, the relationship examined in chapter 10, the student might remind the reader of what they started out wanting to know by writing something like the following:

> This is a study of noneconomic factors related to educational attainment. More specifically, this study examined the relationship between educational attainment and happiness. The general research question was: Do the most educated Americans report being happier than the least educated? Simple contingency table analysis was used to analyze the data which were obtained from the *General Social Survey.*

Following this introduction, the student can then move to what they found out from the study and might write something like the following:

> The main findings of this analysis were:
>
> 1. The data indicate that there is a small but statistically significant relationship between educational attainment and happiness; the greater the

educational attainment, the more likely Americans are to report being happy (table 10.1).
2. The relationship between educational attainment and happiness does not substantially change when controlling for race. Both Black and White Americans with the highest levels of educational attainment report being happier than their counterparts with the lowest levels of educational attainment (tables 10.2 and 10.3).

At this point in the narrative, the student has reminded the reader of the main question of the study—in this example, the relationship between educational attainment and happiness. Following this reminder, she has then reminded the reader of the main findings of the analysis done in chapter 10.

The next step is to address the "So what?" question, that is, to say why the findings are important. Here the student can go back to the justification of the study done in the problem statement chapter. In this example of the educational-attainment-happiness relationship, let us suppose that one justification of the study was to examine the noneconomic outcomes of educational attainment. A good deal has been written about the economic outcomes of higher education, that is, that the more education one has, the more income one is likely to earn over a lifetime. Less work, however, has been done on the noneconomic outcomes of educational attainment. Given this, the student might write something of the order of the following:

This study falls into the category of studies dealing with the noneconomic outcomes of education. Among these are educational attainment's general contribution to individual wellbeing, that is, individual happiness. The data indicate that general happiness is correlated with educational attainment. So, the study suggests that in addition to economic outcomes, higher education also has noneconomic outcomes important for general wellbeing.

Having noted an important noneconomic outcome of education, the next step is for the student to suggest what more research needs to be done, in this example, on the educational-attainment-happiness relationship. One obvious direction for further study is to control for more variables. In general, any study of the correlates of educational attainment—or the correlates of any other social phenomenon for that matter—it is advisable to control for the "big three": race, class, and gender. In the example of the educational-attainment-happiness relationship we have controlled for one of these, namely, race (tables 10.2 and 10.3) but we did not control for class (income) or gender. Accordingly, the student might write something like the following:

More work needs to be done to understand the correlation of educational attainment and happiness. Why are these two things connected? One possibility, of course, might be income. The more education Americans attain, the higher their income. Perhaps the correlation between attainment and happiness is a result their link with income. Further study needs to be done on this. In addition, there still remains the question of whether the correlation found between educational attainment and happiness holds true for both men and women, that is, whether the relationship is affected by gender.

Obviously, if the data are available, all three variables—race, class and gender—as well as others should have been controlled in the study being imagined here. But our purpose here is not to do either a more thorough or sophisticated analysis of data but rather to give a simple example and general idea of the logical progression of a research investigation from the identification and development of a topic to the empirical tests of hypotheses about relationships. The relationships dealt with here have been simple bivariate or two-variable relationships initially, while the suggestion of introducing a third variable (race, in this example) shows how the analysis might proceed as antecedent and intervening variables are considered.

Example: Student Efficacy and Reading Achievement

A similar narrative is applicable to the student-efficacy-reading-achievement example that is also dealt with in chapter 10. As in the educational-attainment-happiness example, the student should begin the fifth chapter of the dissertation—the "Summary, Conclusions, and Recommendations" chapter—by reminding the reader of what she wanted to know about in the first place. In this example, therefore, she might write:

> This purpose of this study was to examine the relationship between between student efficacy and reading achievement. The question addressed was: "Does students' confidence in their reading ability correlate with their reading achievement." More operationally speaking, do fourth-grade NAEP reading scores correlate with students' confidence in their reading ability?

With this introductory paragraph out of the way, the doctoral student can then move to the next step, reporting the principal findings. She might write the following:

> The principal findings of the analysis are:
>
> 1. The data show a statistically significant relationship between fourth-grade students' reading efficacy and their scores on the NAEP assessment. Students with low efficacy scored an average of 181 points out of 500 on the test while students with high efficacy averaged 235, 54 points higher.

2. While there are gender differences in reading achievement—males tend to score lower than females—the differences between males and females with low and high efficacy are roughly similar. For example, there is a 56-point gap between the reading scores of males with low efficacy and those with high efficacy (178 vs. 234). There is a 50-point gap between females with low efficacy and females with high efficacy (186 vs. 236) (tables 10.4 and 10.5).

Having reminded the reader of what she wanted to know and what the data analysis revealed, the doctoral student then can move to the "So what?" step. She might write the following:

The literature on the general relationship between efficacy and performance is extensive and indicates strong, positive associations. This also seems to be the case in the context of education as educational achievement, particularly reading achievement of elementary school students, seems to be influenced by their efficacy. This finding holds implications, in particular, for school counselors who might design interventions to improve student efficacy so as to address the nation's lag in reading scores.

Having addressed the "So what?" question, the doctoral student can then move, as in the educational-attainment-happiness example, to the next step, which is to suggest what further research might be done on the efficacy-reading-achievement relationship. In the analysis of this example in chapter 10, we controlled for gender, one of the "big three." But suggestions of further analysis could include controlling for race and students' family income. In education this often is operationalized by controlling for whether or not the student qualifies for "free and reduced" lunch, a federally funded program.

Summing up, it is in the last chapter of the dissertation that the doctoral student reminds the reader of the primary question of the study, presents the main findings of the analysis—that is, the answer to the primary question—answers the "So what?" question, and suggests directions for further study of the question.

Chapter 12

The Mind's Eye

The general strategy that has been taken here might best be described as a "commonsense" approach to writing the dissertation, an approach that is meant to make the process of doing a dissertation a positive experience, one that results in the development of the mind's eye.

As dealt with in the preceding chapters, the dissertation as understood here consists of five major parts or chapters. Associated with each of these five chapters is one or more commonsense questions.

The first commonsense question that students must ask themselves and answer is simply: "What do I want to know and why is it worth knowing?" The answer to this question is itself a question: it is the primary research question of the study. The primary research question not only begins and ends the dissertation but drives every chapter in between. The primary research question leads to all of the secondary questions and, depending on the methodology, to any research hypotheses. It is the base to which the student must return again and again both to revise as they learn more in the process of writing, and to remind themselves of what it is they want to know.

The second set of commonsense questions has to do with the literature review and conceptual framework. It is about what is already known about the topic of interest and what the student believes he or she will find out from their own research. The questions here are: "Who else has wanted to know what I want to know, what did they find out, and what did they do to find out? Given what they found, what is my best guess about what I am going to find?" The first of these questions is about the knowledge base and of what it consists. The second concerns the conceptual framework of the study.

The third set of commonsense questions has to do with methodology. The question here is simply: "How am I going to find out what I want to know and what am I actually going to do to find out what I want to know?" The answer to this question will have students choosing a research design that will, in turn, have them observe or interview or survey people, or simply sit at a computer, and analyze data or some combination of all of these.

The next commonsense question has to do with data analysis and discussion. Here the question is simply: "What did I find out?" Here the student presents, analyzes, and interprets the data they have collected to help answer their primary research question.

Finally, the commonsense questions that guide the dissertation's final summary-conclusions-and-recommendation chapter are: "What did I start out want to know?" "What did I find out?" "So what?" and "What more needs to be done?"

These commonsense questions are meant to help the student keep an overview of the project as they work on the many details it requires. They are meant to serve as reminders of what needs to be done and why it needs to be done.

In conjunction with these commonsense questions are practical and theoretical questions. The introduction of these two types of questions is meant to help the student keep the practical or applied end of the research distinct from the theoretical side. The theoretical questions are especially important as aids to the formulation of the research problem itself. Formulating the research problem is the process of subjecting a "topic" to the various theoretical questions. This process should produce not only the research problem but lay the groundwork for the conceptual framework as well.

In sum, this book is an effort to introduce doctoral students to the practice of asking and answering some commonsense and practical-theoretical questions about their research topics and dissertations. The aim throughout has been to make the dissertation experience a positive and productive one that ends with the doctoral degree in hand. When this is achieved, however, the result will not only be a piece of paper but a transformation of mind itself.

One cannot write a doctoral dissertation with changing oneself in the process, without sharpening the mind's eye. The process of doing a dissertation from start to finish will transform how one looks at the world and oneself as well. Having been through the thought processes involved in doing a dissertation, students will view the world differently. They will be able to see complexity and detail that previously remained invisible to them and others who lack their mental training. They will also likely find that in doing the dissertation without losing their mind, they have developed their mental capacity in ways that help them acquire new knowledge more efficiently and effectively than they could have done without the dissertation experience. Apart from any financial gains this enhanced ability may bring—and it will likely bring some—it is rewarding in itself.

Appendix A
Accessing the GSS and NAEP Data

The National Opinion Research Center (NORC) is the main website for information about and access to the *General Social Survey* (GSS) and it can be found here: https://gss.norc.org/. From this site one can scroll down on the right to the "Quick Links" and find the *GSS Data Explorer link*: https://gssdataexplorer.norc.org/home. Clicking on the "Tour Guide" will provide an overview of the functions available.

The NORC website, however, is not the only way to access the GSS. An alternative method is via the *SDA: Survey Documentation and Analysis* site run by the University of California at Berkeley. This is the site used for the analysis in this book and it can be accessed via SDA: Survey Documentation and Analysis (https://sda.berkeley.edu/). Students should examine both sites and decide which they find more accessible.

Keeping with the UC Berkeley site, clicking on https://sda.berkeley.edu/ takes one to the page shown in figure A.1:

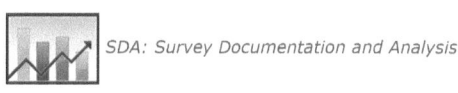
SDA: Survey Documentation and Analysis

Home Archive Community Documentation Projects News

SDA is a set of programs for the documentation and Web-based analysis of survey data. SDA was developed, distributed and supported by the Computer-assisted Survey Methods Program (CSM) at the University of California, Berkeley until the end of 2014. Beginning in 2015, CSM is managed and supported by the Institute for Scientific Analysis, a private, non-profit organization, under an exclusive continuing license agreement with the University of California. CSM also develops the CASES software package.

To see how it all works, test-drive SDA at our demonstration SDA Archive. Browse the documentation for a survey and get *fast* data analysis results. The SDA Archive includes several datasets, including the **General Social Survey (GSS)**, the **American National Election Study (ANES)**, and the **Survey of Consumer Finances (SCF)**. You can also look at some other archives that use SDA software.

For information on obtaining SDA software and services, see the SDA Software and Services **page.**

For video tutorials on using the SDA 4 user interface see the SDA YouTube Channel.

SDA Features

Figure A.1: The SDA: Survey documentation and analysis page

Appendix A

From this page, students should click on "Archive," which will take them to a page at which they need to SCROLL DOWN until they see the following list of data:

General Social Surveys (GSS)

November 21, 2023: the GSS Cumulative Datafile 1972-2022 (release 2) has been added below.

(Abst) | General Social Survey (GSS) Cumulative Datafile 1972-2022 - release 2 (SDA 4) New release!
(Abst) | General Social Survey (GSS) Cumulative Datafile 1972-2021 - release 3b (SDA 4)
(Abst) | General Social Survey (GSS) Cumulative Datafile 1972-2021 - release 1a (SDA 4)
(Abst) | General Social Survey (GSS) Cumulative Datafile 1972-2018 - release 1 (SDA 4) | (SDA 3.5) | (Quick Tables)
(Abst) | General Social Survey (GSS) Cumulative Datafile 1972-2016 - release 1 (SDA 4) | (SDA 3.5) | (Quick Tables)
(Abst) | General Social Survey (GSS) Cumulative Datafile 1972-2014 - release 2 (SDA 4) | (SDA 3.5) | (Quick Tables)
(Abst) | General Social Survey (GSS) Cumulative Datafile 1972-2012 (SDA 4) | (SDA 3.5) | (Quick Tables)
(Abst) | General Social Survey (GSS) Cumulative Datafile 1972-2010 (SDA 4) | (SDA 3.5) | (Quick Tables)
(Abst) | General Social Survey (GSS) Cumulative Datafile 1972-2008 (SDA 4) | (SDA 3.5) | (Quick Tables)
(Abst) | General Social Survey (GSS) Cumulative Datafile 1972-2006 (SDA 4) | (SDA 3.5) | (Quick Tables)
(Abst) | General Social Survey Panel (2006 Sample) Wave 3 (SDA 4) | (SDA 3.5)

Figure A.2: List of data sets available on the SDA archive page

Once they arrive at this list, students should click on the first data file: "(ABST) General Social Survey (GSS) Cumulative Datafile 1972–2022 -release 2 (SDA 4) *New release.* Clicking on this data file will take students to the main data analysis page shown in figure A.3.

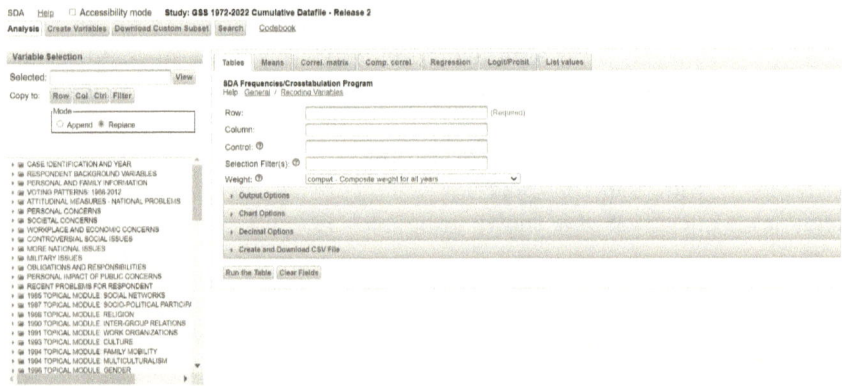

Figure A.3: Main analysis page for the SDA Berkeley site GSS

This is the page on which students can do all their analyses. The page has two sides. On the left side of the page is the list of variables that can be viewed via the dropdown arrows. The right side is for analyzing variables. But focusing first on the left side, clicking on "RESPONDENT BACKGROUND VARIABLES" drops down a menu containing the following variables: "age, gender, race, and ethnicity" of the respondents in the survey. Clicking on that down arrow reveals a list of variables the first three of which are "age," "sex," and "race." Clicking on, say, "sex," put this variable name in the selection window at the top left. Clicking on the "view" link brings up the page shown below in figure A.4. Then, clicking on the "x" in the lower right corner hides this window.

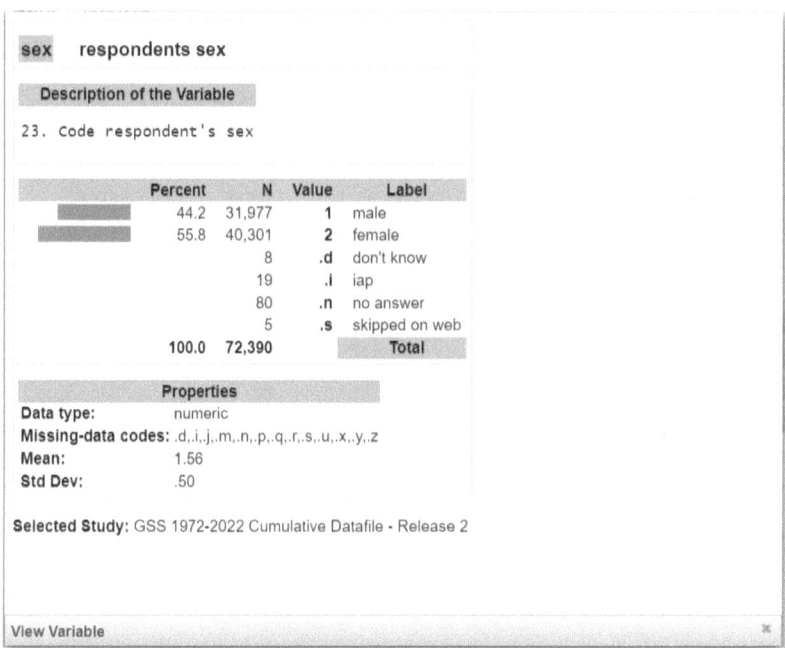

Figure A.4: Pop-up from view variables selection window

If students then click on the "row" link under the "Variable Selection" window, the variable "sex" then appears on the right side of the window in the "Row" window of the "SDA Frequencies/Crosstabulation Program." Clicking on the "Run the Table" link at the bottom of this side of the window produces the output frequency output below.

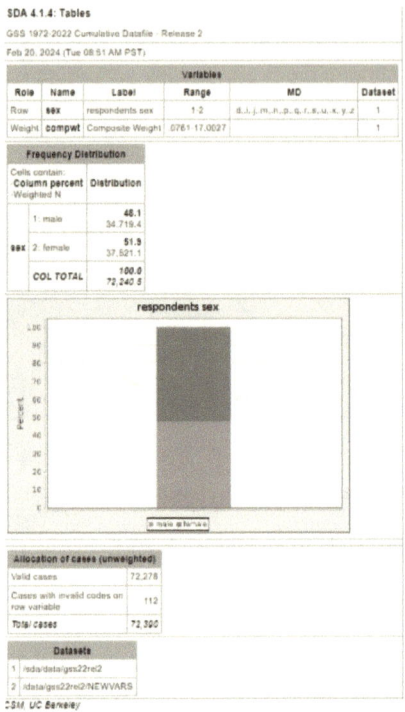

Figure A.5: Frequency output from SDA Berkeley GSS analysis page

Students can also choose "output," "chart," and "decimal" options to refine the output.

If students find the SDA Berkeley a bit daunting, they should use the NORC site to analyze their data. Some students, however, may find both sites useful for different purposes.

ACCESSING THE NAEP DATA

Students can find the NAEP data by Googling "NAEP Data Explorer" and clicking on the appropriate search result. Doing so should bring them to the page below shown in figure A.6.

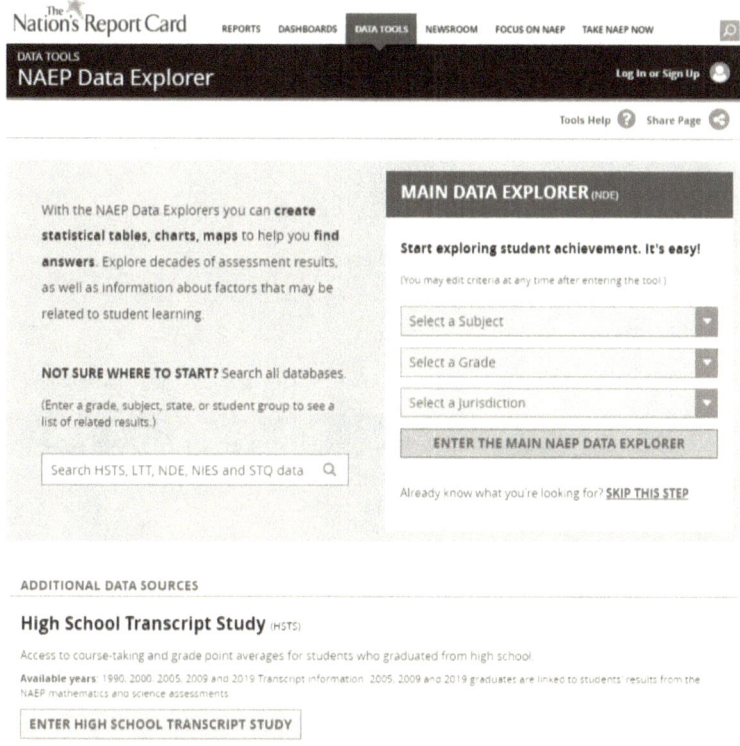

Figure A.6: Main NAEP data explorer page

From this point, students should select a subject, grade and jurisdiction from the dropdown windows. For this book, the subject has been "reading," for "grade 4" and the jurisdiction has been "national public" schools. Upon making these selections, students are then able to click on the link, "ENTER THE MAIN NAEP DATA EXPLORER." After agreeing accept the rules and restrictions, students will then see the page below shown in figure A.7. From here, students only need choose the variables that they wish to explore and their related statistics.

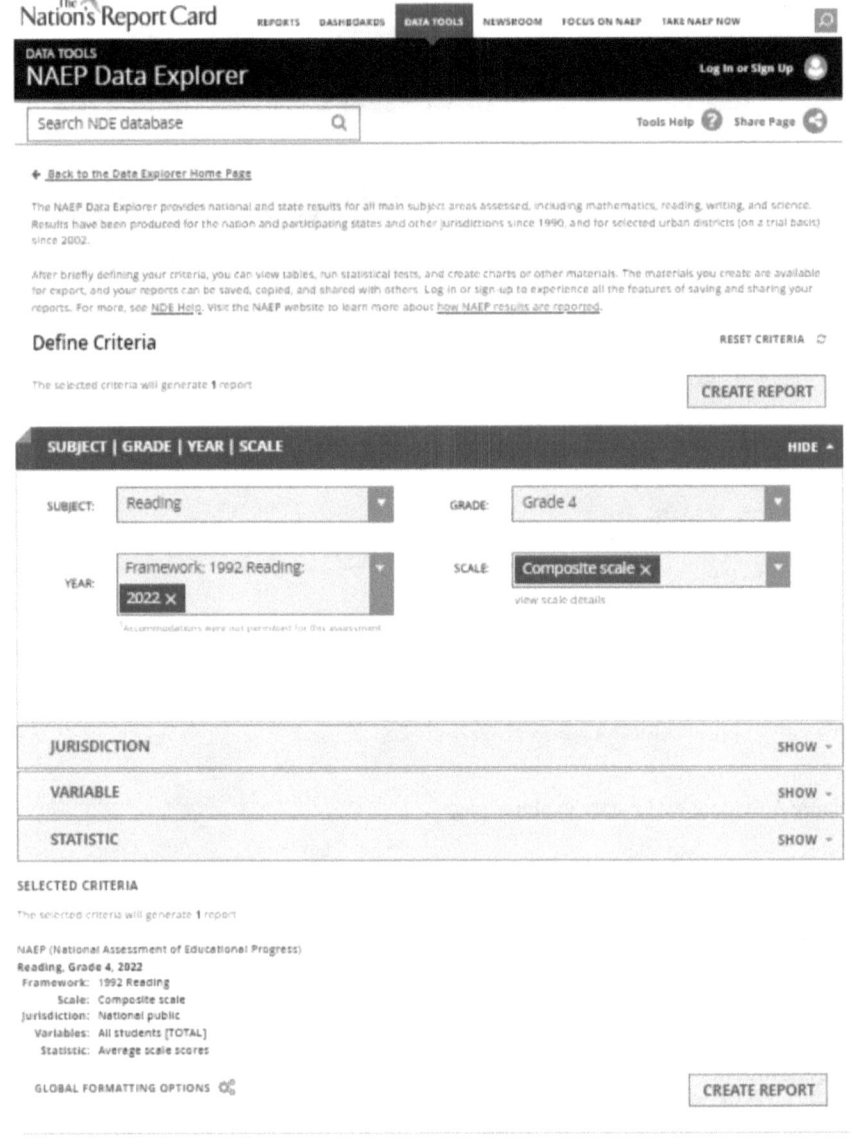

Figure A.7: Main NAEP data explorer analysis page

References

Almeida, Daniel, Andrew M. Byrne, Rachel M. Smith, and Saul Ruiz. "How Relevant Is Grit? The Importance of Social Capital in First-Generation College Students Academic Success." *Journal of College Student Retention: Research, Theory & Practice* 23, no. 3 (2021): 539–59.

Anderson, Lorin W., et al. *A Taxonomy for Learning, Teaching, and Assessing: A Revision of Bloom's Taxonomy of Educational Objectives.* Longman, 2001.

Burgess, Hilary, Sandy Sieminski, and Lori Arthur. *Achieving Your Doctorate in Education.* Thousand Oaks, CA: Sage, 2006.

Cormier-Zenon, Dolores E. "Can Parental Expectations Compensate for the Negative Effects of Low Birth Weight on Academic Achievement: A Cross-Sectional Analysis of the National PEELS Data." EdD diss. The University of Louisiana at Lafayette, 2012.

Fountain, Jason M. "Differences in Generational Work Values in America and Their Implications for Educational Leadership: A Longitudinal Test of Twenge's Model." EdD diss. The University of Louisiana at Lafayette, 2014.

Gall, Meredith D., Joyce P. Gall, and Walter Borg. *Educational Research: An Introduction*, 8th ed. Boston: Pearson, 2007.

Glaser, Barney, and Anselm Strauss. *The Discovery of Grounded Theory.* New York: Routledge, 1999.

Lau, Chun. "Exploring the Relationship between Educational Attainment and Political Participation," EdD Dissertation, The University of Louisiana at Lafayette, 2023.

Lubisi, Anathi, and Fhulu H. Nekhwevha. "Effects of Family Background on Poor Academic Performance of Grade 12 Learners." *International Journal of Social Science Research and Review* 7, no. 1 (2024): 270–77.

McCallen, Leigh S., and Helen L. Johnson. "The Role of Institutional Agents in Promoting Higher Education Success among First-Generation College Students at a Public Urban University." *Journal of Diversity in Higher Education* 13, no. 4 (2020): 320–32.

National Center for Education Statistics. "The Nation's Report Card," U.S. Department of Education, 2024. https://www.nationsreportcard.gov/faq.aspx

Phillips, D. C. *A Companion to John Dewey's Democracy and Education.* Chicago: University of Chicago Press, 2016.

Twenge, J. M. "A Review of the Empirical Evidence on Generational Differences in Work Attitudes." *Journal of Business Psychology* 25 (2010): 201–10.

About the Author

Robert O. Slater is a professor of education who does research and writes on educational leadership, democracy, and human development in K–12 and higher education. He received his BA from the Harris Teachers College in St. Louis, MO, one of the historic HBCUs in the United States; his MEd from Harvard University in Cambridge, MA; and his PhD from the University of Chicago in Chicago, IL. He was a Fulbright scholar to Peru in 1996, to Bolivia in 2010, and to Greece in 2018. He taught at the University of Maryland, Louisiana State University, and Texas A&M before joining the faculty at the University of Louisiana at Lafayette in 2007. He has lectured on educational leadership, democracy, and human development at the Catholic University in Lima, Peru, as well as the Catholic University in Lapaz, Bolivia. From 1986–1988 he was a senior research associate at the US Department of Education in Washington, D.C., where he directed the department's educational research initiatives. Dr. Slater is a member of the American Educational Research Association (AERA), the American Psychological Association (APA), and the American Sociological Association (ASA).

www.ingramcontent.com/pod-product-compliance
Lightning Source LLC
Chambersburg PA
CBHW032216230426
43672CB00011B/2579